TOBACCO CONTROL LAWS

Implementation and Enforcement

PETER D. JACOBSON

JEFFREY WASSERMAN

Supported by
The Robert Wood Johnson Foundation

RAND

PREFACE

This report was developed under a grant from The Robert Wood Johnson Foundation's Substance Abuse Policy Research Program. In this project, RAND assessed the implementation and enforcement of tobacco control laws in seven states. For tobacco control legislation to be an effective public policy approach, the implementation and enforcement of the laws must be diffused to the public, to business establishments, and to tobacco vendors. Understanding the process of diffusion, and especially barriers to enforcement or implementation, will assist policymakers, legislators, and interested stakeholders in designing an effective anti-tobacco strategy. This document should therefore be of interest to federal, state, and local legislators and health policymakers; tobacco control advocates and other health care stakeholders; and health policy researchers.

CONTENTS

TABLES

SUMMARY

INTRODUCTION

In recent years, many states and localities have enacted laws restricting smoking in public places. Despite the large number of such laws, little empirical research has assessed the manner in which these laws are implemented and enforced. The dearth of research in this area is especially troublesome in view of several recent studies indicating that laws and ordinances restricting smoking in public places can be an effective tobacco control strategy (Wasserman et al., 1991; Chaloupka, 1988; Keeler et al., 1991), and that rigorous enforcement of youth access laws can reduce teenagers' access to cigarettes (Feighery, Altman, and Shaffer, 1991; Jason et al., 1991).

The purpose of this study is to examine, through a series of detailed case studies, the process by which tobacco control laws and ordinances are implemented and enforced by state and local authorities. For legislation to be an effective public policy approach, the implementation and enforcement of the laws must be diffused to the public, to business establishments, and to tobacco vendors. Understanding the process of diffusion, and especially barriers to enforcement or implementation, will assist policymakers, legislators, and interested stakeholders in designing an effective anti-tobacco strategy.

This study was designed to address the following research questions:

- How are anti-tobacco laws—both those related to clean indoor air and teen access—implemented and enforced at the state and local levels?

- What is the effect of strong statewide anti-tobacco legislation on the development and implementation of local anti-tobacco ordinances?
- What role does an anti-tobacco coalition play once statewide legislation is enacted?
- What strategy has the tobacco industry adopted in response to the implementation and enforcement of anti-tobacco laws?
- What are the most effective legislative/regulatory/policy strategies given the results of this study?

We also address the following specific issues: the process by which anti-tobacco laws and ordinances are diffused throughout the community; the effects of such laws in the absence of a strong enforcement mechanism; the relationship between statewide laws and local ordinances; the relative effectiveness of various legislative provisions, especially those limiting teenage access to cigarettes; the role of anti-tobacco coalitions in seeing that laws enacted are adequately enforced; whether these laws are merely symbolic legislative statements as opposed to meaningful policy options for preventing exposure to environmental tobacco smoke and reducing teenage smoking initiation rates and cigarette consumption; the barriers to effective diffusion; the process of diffusing anti-tobacco restrictions across communities within a state; and how information about anti-tobacco restrictions is disseminated to the public.

At the heart of our conceptual approach are three complementary theses, based on our previous research and review of the literature, about the legislative and implementation processes. The first is that it is easier for anti-tobacco advocates to organize around the enactment of legislation than it is to sustain the momentum to monitor the implementation and enforcement of anti-tobacco laws. Second, absent a strong enforcement mechanism, statewide anti-tobacco legislation may represent a mere symbolic statement about the state's desire to control smoking that is dependent on people's good will for success. Such statements, however, may produce attitudinal and behavioral change on the part of individuals. And finally, efforts by state and local anti-tobacco coalitions will be integral to successful enforcement and implementation of any anti-tobacco laws.

METHODOLOGY

Although it would have been desirable to review state laws and local ordinances in every state, resource constraints prevented such an ambitious agenda. Instead, we limited our case study sites to seven states: California, Arizona, Texas, New York, Minnesota, Illinois, and Florida. These include the six states from our previous study of the political evolution of anti-tobacco legislation (Jacobson, Wasserman, and Raube, 1993) plus California. These states represent a mix of legal environments across several dimensions. Some have strong statewide legislation and weak local ordinances (Minnesota), others have the reverse (Texas), and one has strong statewide and local anti-tobacco laws (New York). The states also vary in their approaches to vending machine and sample distribution restrictions.

In addition, we visited a number of local sites within each state. Selection criteria for the local sites included community size, geographic location, type and strength of the ordinances, and duration of the ordinances.

Before conducting the site visits, we developed a semi-structured interview protocol. The protocol was designed to elicit discussion about the following specific topics: (1) recent or current tobacco control initiatives; (2) implementation and enforcement strategies, along with changes in strategies over time; (3) stakeholder roles in enforcement and implementation; (4) the relationship between statewide anti-tobacco legislation and local ordinances; (5) how anti-tobacco coalitions organize and operate to facilitate implementation and enforcement; and (6) barriers to effective enforcement, including tobacco industry responses to enforcement and implementation efforts.

In each state, we interviewed local and state enforcement agency officials and representatives of affected businesses (and their associations), such as restaurants, convenience stores, and other tobacco vendors. We met with leaders of anti-tobacco advocacy groups, voluntary health organizations (such as the American Cancer Society, American Lung Association, and the American Heart Association), and, where possible, officials and attorneys for the tobacco industry. The interview targets were selected based on discussions with our contacts in each state and based on the need to provide specific information about the implementation and enforcement process.

Our analysis of the case studies focuses on synthesizing the results of our document reviews and interviews and on extracting a set of cross-cutting themes, or lessons, that can be applied by legislators, other policymakers, and anti-tobacco advocates. The primary form of analysis is descriptive, comparing and contrasting information across sites along several dimensions of interest. These dimensions include levels of enforcement at the state and local levels; the process by which the tobacco control initiative is diffused to the public; the role of interest groups, specifically anti-tobacco coalitions and the tobacco industry; and barriers to effective implementation.

RESULTS

How Are Tobacco Control Laws Implemented and Enforced?

During our interviews, respondents consistently distinguished between implementation and enforcement. Enforcement relates to the narrow range of potential sanctions contained in state legislation or local ordinances, such as license removal, fines, or other penalties resulting from specific law enforcement activity. On the one hand, enforcement refers to actions required by law that are monitored by state and local officials. On the other hand, implementation is viewed by respondents as a much broader term, encompassing educational activities, dissemination of materials by stakeholders, and developing processes to ensure compliance with state and local tobacco control laws.

State-Level Enforcement. The overwhelming consensus of our interviews is that state clean indoor air laws are self-enforcing and that they will not be systematically enforced by state or local authorities. By self-enforcing, we mean that people voluntarily comply with the law in the absence of a proactive enforcement effort.

In our sample, enforcement of state clean indoor air laws is delegated to local health departments in all states except California. The ironic result is that we observed little difference in state-level activity between states with strong statewide anti-tobacco laws, states that preempt stronger local ordinances, and states with no statewide anti-tobacco legislation.

Local-Level Enforcement. The willingness and ability of local agencies to enforce state clean indoor air laws vary in our sample but are generally quite limited. A major concern expressed by local health departments in New York, Minnesota, California, and Illinois is that this amounts to an unfunded mandate. Thus, few local agencies actively enforce state clean indoor air laws beyond responding to complaints.

In several instances, including the city of Chicago and Suffolk and Chatauqua Counties in New York, local health departments have opted to enforce their own local ordinances instead of the state law. But like their state counterparts, local agencies consistently rely on voluntary compliance. As with the state clean indoor air laws, these local ordinances are self-enforcing.

In contrast to the implementation and enforcement of the clean indoor air laws, states and localities in our sample have been much more aggressive in enforcing laws restricting youth access to tobacco. Perhaps the primary difference is a consistent belief that teen access laws will not be self-enforcing, thus requiring a greater enforcement effort than what is needed for clean indoor air regulations. The applicable regulatory question is what mechanisms work best to limit youth access to tobacco products.

Relationship Between Statewide Legislation and Local Ordinances

A critical strategy decision faced by tobacco control advocates is whether to focus their efforts at the state or local level. This decision presents a clear trade-off. Thus, statewide legislation offers the prospect of enacting a law that provides a uniform level of protection, in the case of clean indoor air, to all of the state's residents. Ideally, from the anti-tobacco advocates' point of view, the law would be quite stringent and would also provide local communities with the option of increasing the level of stringency by passing local ordinances (i.e., the law would not contain any preemption provisions). Such a strategy provides an efficient and effective route to both controlling smoking in a wide range of public places, including private work sites, and reducing minors' access to tobacco.

The downside of this strategy is that, as we saw repeatedly in our seven case studies, the tobacco industry possesses substantial political power at the state level and has been enormously successful in either turning back bills that they consider to be contrary to their interests or by insisting that any state bill include a preemption clause, such as those found in the Illinois and Florida clean indoor air bills.

Suffice it to say that the debate among anti-tobacco advocates on the preferred legislative strategy is far from settled. In our case studies, however, it became evident that a complex interplay exists between statewide and local laws, with each influencing the prospects and shape of the other. We found, for instance, with the exception of some downstate New York counties, that local communities were generally not inclined to pass clean indoor air ordinances in states that had enacted statewide laws, even if there were no preemption clauses in the bill that would have prevented them from doing so.

The issue of enforcement is a central concern in evaluating the relative merits of a statewide versus a local tobacco control strategy. Based on our site visits, we believe that local enforcement is a critical ingredient to the success of virtually any tobacco control effort, regardless of whether it revolves around clean indoor air or teen access. This is not to say that local ordinances are preferred to statewide legislation, but merely that statewide laws should include a local enforcement component.

Stakeholder Roles in Enforcement and Implementation

Anti-Tobacco Coalitions. Three distinct themes characterize our interviews with anti-tobacco coalitions. First, coalitions are organized around legislation. Their interest in implementation and enforcement is secondary. Instead, government agencies play the central role in implementation and enforcement efforts. Second, involvement in implementation and enforcement tends to be on youth access restrictions rather than on clean indoor air regulations. Third, all of the coalitions discuss the importance of community education but tend to do so in vague, general terms, rather than presenting a coherent educational program with defined objectives.

The Tobacco Industry. Although the tobacco industry continues to play a dominant role in legislative matters, our results suggest that the industry plays a minor role in enforcement and implementation once laws are enacted. To be sure, the industry tries to limit the effectiveness of tobacco control legislation by restricting the range of potential enforcement sanctions, but we found no evidence that the tobacco industry is involved in the process of implementing or enforcing the laws.

Retail Merchants. Our interviews revealed considerable variation in the involvement of retail merchants associations in tobacco control enforcement and implementation. For the most part, retail merchants associations do not appear to be involved in enforcement and implementation activities, but the Illinois Retail Merchants Association (IRMA) is actively engaged in monitoring enforcement efforts. Coalitions reported almost no interaction with retail merchants. Government agencies indicated that retail merchants associations were cooperative but rarely went beyond providing general information and, sometimes, signs to members for display in stores. Not all associations in our sample provided informational materials to members, and of those states in our sample only Illinois (IRMA) had provided training or education to members.

Barriers to Effective Implementation and Enforcement

We focused a considerable portion of our discussions with the respondents on identifying barriers to the effective implementation and enforcement of tobacco control laws at the state and local levels. Several unmistakable themes emerged that cut across states, local communities, and even type of tobacco control law (i.e., teen access or clean indoor air). One such theme we found particularly surprising: The relative salience of the smoking issue appeared to be low in comparison with other public policy issues.

Implicitly or explicitly, respondents indicated that tobacco control often failed to ignite the passions of state legislators or city council members or even of the public at large. Many expressed their disappointment about the apparent unwillingness of elected officials and others to work tirelessly on enacting, implementing, and enforcing increasingly stringent anti-tobacco measures.

A second barrier to more effective implementation and enforcement frequently cited by respondents was resource constraints. The lack of adequate resources for implementation efforts has resulted in delays in enforcing the law and confusion on the parts of businesses and other affected parties. On the enforcement side, inadequate resources have meant that many states and local communities have undertaken no systematic and/or proactive initiatives to enforce tobacco control laws, but rather have relied on "systems" that are almost exclusively complaint-driven. Although the presence of strong social norms against exposing individuals to passive smoke have by and large obviated the need for states and locales to actively enforce clean indoor air laws, all evidence indicates that teen access laws are decidedly not self-enforcing and that ongoing so-called "sting" operations are essential to maintaining low illegal sales rates.

Discussion and Recommendations

Relationship Between Legislative Enactment, Implementation, and Enforcement. During the course of this project, it became clear that the distinction between enactment and implementation/enforcement made by many observers is an artificial one, and that in a very real sense, the two are inextricably linked. Specifically, many of the respondents argued that the enactment process itself—particularly in instances where that process was protracted—served to change attitudes and social norms regarding the importance of tobacco control measures. At least for the clean indoor air measures, these changed social norms paved the way for a smooth implementation process and minimized the need to embark on a vigorous enforcement effort, thus leaving these laws to be primarily self-enforcing. We found, however, that the strength of this relationship decreased when it came to teen access laws.

Effective Enforcement Mechanisms. An overwhelming majority of respondents made the same recommendation regarding increasing the effectiveness of various enforcement mechanisms: Keep them simple. This recommendation applied to both clean indoor air and teen access measures. Moreover, the respondents recommended that all aspects of the enforcement mechanism—including where authority is vested, the structure of the penalties, the person within the establishment who will be penalized, etc.—be detailed in the legislation or ordinance.

Clean Indoor Air. As we have already mentioned, clean indoor air laws are for the most part self-enforcing in the sense that people are generally made aware of the law through a variety of educational programs and media campaigns and, in those rare instances where infractions occur, are reminded by others that smoking is not permitted. If an individual smoker or establishment refuses to comply with the law, then an administrative penalty should be imposed on the offending party.

A second recommendation aimed at increasing the effectiveness of clean indoor air laws is that criteria for defining or characterizing establishments should be clearly articulated in either the laws themselves or in the accompanying regulations. It is particularly critical to clearly distinguish restaurants from bars, as the latter are often exempt from clean indoor air laws.

Finally, an effort should be made to minimize the number of exceptions to the law, since failure to do so will require costly hearings and present tricky enforcement problems. As the number of exceptions grows, the probability of violations appears to increase: Tobacco merchants can maintain that the law does not apply to their establishments because they fall into an exempt category.

Youth Access. Our case study results make it abundantly clear that an ongoing enforcement effort—complete with routine compliance checks—is essential for reducing the rate of illegal cigarette sales to minors. Additionally, we found that to be effective, local ordinances must have a graduated penalty structure that starts with a moderate fine for the first offense and escalates in severity with each subsequent offense.

We also believe that licensing cigarette vendors at the local level is a critical ingredient to an effective enforcement program, for two reasons. First, as we observed in several Minnesota locales, license fees can be used to finance regular compliance checks, thus making the enforcement effort economically self-sufficient. This, in turn, will ensure its long-run survival. Second, license suspension for varying periods of time, depending on the number of prior offenses, should be an integral component of the ordinance's penalty structure, because even substantial fines may, in some instances, fail to provide a substantial deterrent to illegal sales. For chronic offenders, license revocation should also be an option.

Absence of a State-Level Enforcement Strategy by Anti-Tobacco Advocates

To some extent, the lack of commitment that anti-tobacco forces have shown toward implementation and enforcement issues is a reflection of the fact that their resources are being directed toward enacting tobacco control ordinances at the local level and fighting tobacco industry–led attempts to pass state-level legislation that preempts local tobacco control ordinances. This diversion of resources is the direct result of the tobacco industry's strategy to focus its attention at the state level and, specifically, on preemption. By substantially reducing, if not eliminating, the prospects of passing stringent statewide legislation, this strategy has essentially raised the costs faced by anti-tobacco activists to enact, implement, and enforce tobacco control measures.

Symbolic Statements and Cultural Change

Some commentators have hypothesized that the vagueness of most statewide legislation and concomitant limitations in enforcement authority render statewide legislation more of a symbolic statement of intention to control smoking than an easily enforceable mandate. Even when enacted, these laws are subject to legal challenge and are not self-executing. In contrast, local ordinances are likely to be enforced by local authorities who may be more accountable to anti-tobacco coalition pressure (Jacobson, Wasserman, and Raube, 1993; Samuels et al., 1992; Samuels and Glantz, 1991). Our results suggest that this is accurate for clean indoor air laws, but not for youth access restrictions. Most respondents agreed that the clean indoor air acts will be self-executing through community values, but that only the prospect of fines and license forfeiture makes youth access restrictions enforceable.

Lessons for Other Public Health Measures

Legislation will continue to be a primary battleground for public health issues ranging from gun control to motorcycle helmets. When considering what compromises to accept to achieve specified legislative goals, public health advocates need to consider the locus of enforcement responsibility and the sanctions available to the enforcement agency. Our results do not augur well for state-level enforcement of public health measures that are opposed by powerful and politically well-connected interests. Public health advocates should ensure that local agencies have adequate enforcement responsibility and powers. As both the literature and our results suggest, legislation and implementation are intertwined. In particular, effective enforcement is linked to legislation that provides specific enforcement mechanisms, such as license removal. To the extent that a given public health measure is likely to be self-enforcing, these issues will be less critical.

ACKNOWLEDGMENTS

We would like to express our sincere thanks to a number of individuals for contributing their support to this project. David Altman, who serves as National Program Director for The Robert Wood Johnson Foundation's Substance Abuse Policy Research Program, provided general oversight on the project and was helpful in increasing the project's visibility among researchers and the health policy community. Russell Sciandra and RAND colleague Mark Spranca provided insightful comments on an earlier draft of this report, and Ruth Eagle-Winsick did an excellent job in preparing the manuscript for publication. We are also grateful for the research assistance that John Anderson provided and for the editorial assistance provided by Christina Pitcher. In addition, we would like to thank all of the people who allowed us to interview them for this project. Without their full cooperation, the project would not have been possible. A number of these individuals also agreed to review drafts of the state case studies for technical accuracy. Finally, we would like to thank the staff and board of The Robert Wood Johnson Foundation for providing the financial support required to conduct this research.

Chapter One

INTRODUCTION

In recent years, many states and localities have enacted laws restricting smoking in public places and youth access to tobacco products. Despite the large number of such laws, little empirical research has assessed or evaluated the manner in which these laws are implemented and enforced. The dearth of research in this area is especially troublesome in view of several recent studies indicating that laws and ordinances restricting smoking in public places can be an effective tobacco control strategy (Wasserman et al., 1991; Chaloupka, 1988; Keeler et al., 1991), and that rigorous enforcement of youth access laws can in fact reduce teenagers' access to tobacco (Feighery, Altman, and Shaffer, 1991; Jason et al., 1991).

The purpose of this study is to examine, through a series of detailed case studies, the process by which tobacco control laws and ordinances are implemented and enforced by state and local authorities. For legislation to be an effective public policy approach, the implementation and enforcement of the laws must be diffused to the public, to business establishments, and to tobacco product vendors. Understanding the process of diffusion, and especially barriers to enforcement or implementation, will assist policymakers, legislators, and interested stakeholders in designing an effective anti-tobacco strategy.

Tobacco control legislation is designed to achieve certain policy objectives, usually the protection of nonsmokers from environmental tobacco smoke (ETS) and often limiting teenage access to tobacco. Enacting statewide and local tobacco control measures is a necessary, though not sufficient, condition for ensuring that smokers and nonsmokers alike can enjoy a smoke-free environment when frequenting public places and that teenagers are denied easy access to tobacco. Enactment of these tobacco control measures does not imply that they will be implemented effectively and enforced rigorously. Consequently, it is misleading to assume that the mere passage of tobacco control legislation and ordinances will result in smoke-free public places and/or decreased teenage smoking initiation rates.

Without closer scrutiny of how the legislation is implemented and enforced, it is difficult to determine whether the legislative policy objectives are being met. One issue, for example, is whether statewide anti-tobacco legislation is merely a symbolic statement of legislative concern for controlling smoking rather than an easily enforceable mandate. Second, very little is known about the relationship between state and local tobacco control regulations. How does the implementation and enforcement of statewide anti-tobacco legislation affect the enactment and enforcement of local ordinances? Third, little is known about the effects of enacting anti-tobacco ordinances in one locality on decisions to enact smoking restrictions in geographically proximate communities. Fourth, what are the components of an effective implementation and enforcement effort? Fifth, what role do anti-tobacco coalitions play in implementation and enforcement?

BACKGROUND

The History of Regulation

The use and regulation of tobacco is one of the most controversial public policy topics at all levels of government. From a regulatory perspective, the principal conundrum is how to regulate a product that is lethal when used as intended but remains legal for people over 18 years of age. As such, tobacco control reveals some of the most salient tensions in American political theory: Under what circumstances can government limit individual freedoms to protect citizens from the consequences of their personal and lifestyle choices? What is the relationship between the federal, state, and local governments as the centers of regulatory responsibility for controlling tobacco use? How can conflicting rights and interests (e.g., the right to avoid cigarette smoke versus the right to smoke) best be resolved? And what role do social norms play in discouraging smoking in public places relative to tobacco control laws?

Even today, when smoking in public places is highly regulated in many states, the debate over the scope of that regulation is far from settled. The tension between individual liberties and governmental intervention to protect the public's health is at issue. That the state has the power to regulate smoking to secure the public's health is beyond question. The policy debate is about when, how, and under what circumstances the state should exercise that power (Jacobson, Wasserman, and Raube, 1993).

Historical Antecedents. Despite a few 17th century restrictions, significant anti-tobacco legislation was not enacted until the second half of the 19th century, primarily in response to the fire hazard created by smoking. Two themes characterized this early legislation: One theme focused on the fire hazard created by smoking, while the other concentrated on the morality of smoking. Eventually, opposition to smoking on moral grounds was swept aside by the economic benefits associated with tobacco production and consumption. As the popularity of smoking grew, states realized that cigarette taxes were an important source of revenue, so early anti-tobacco legislation was repealed. In fact, by 1927 all state statutes were repealed and the anti-tobacco movement was legally, as well as practically, dead. The political tide did not begin to turn again until the 1960s and lacked momentum until the 1980s.

Opposition to Smoking on Moral Grounds. In 1856–57, the British medical journal *Lancet* featured an issue in which 50 doctors expressed their views on "The Great Tobacco Question." Various doctors associated tobacco with increases in crime, nervous paralysis, loss of intellectual capacity, and vision impairment. But the *Lancet* editors argued that since tobacco use was so widespread, it must have some good or at least pleasurable effects. If the evil effects of tobacco were as dreadful as these doctors claimed, the journal's editors concluded that the human race would have ceased to exist (Wagner, 1971; Kluger, 1996).

By the late 1800s, many observers thought cigarettes were corrupt and morally repugnant. For example, in 1884, *The New York Times* warned that smoking could "ruin the republic." Women who smoked were considered promiscuous and were warned they could become sterile, mustachioed, or tuberculous. In the 1890s, Lucy Page Gaston led a Chicago-based anti-tobacco campaign modeled on the anti-alcohol campaign. Similarly, Henry Ford spoke against smoking, and Thomas Edison refused to hire smokers (Wagner, 1971; Kluger, 1996).

At the beginning of the 20th century, 14 states had passed laws banning the production, sale, advertisement, or use of cigarettes within their boundaries. For example, in 1897, Tennessee adopted a statute to prohibit the sale of cigarettes. The statute was upheld by the Tennessee and United States Supreme Courts as a valid exercise of a state's police power to protect public health (*Austin v. Tennessee,* 179 U.S. 472 (1900)). In 1901, New Hampshire made it illegal for any person, firm, or corporation to produce, sell, or store for sale any form of cigarette. A 1907 Illinois law made the manufacture, sale, or gift of a cigarette punishable by a fine of not more than $100 or jail for not more than 30 days. In New York, women were forbidden to smoke in public. Progressive reformers in the early 20th century were particularly concerned about the "demoralizing" effects of tobacco on children, leading to laws prohibiting tobacco sales (primarily cigarettes) to children under the age of 18 (or 21) in many states (IOM, 1994).

As smoking grew in popularity, the laws were not enforced and, in many instances, were ultimately repealed. By 1909, when the last of these early state laws were passed, national cigarette sales were twice what they had been five years earlier. Cigarette smoking increased dramatically from 1930 on, with the greatest percentage of gains during and immediately following World War II. In 1945, 267 billion cigarettes were sold, 12 percent more than in 1944, 48 percent more than in 1940, and 124 percent more than in 1930 (Wagner, 1971).

Opposition to Smoking on Health Grounds. Accompanying this growth in the popularity of smoking, scientific evidence regarding its ill effects began to be published. In the 1930s, the medical community began to investigate the increase in lung cancer, and by the 1940s, scientific reports began to associate smoking with cancer, heart disease, and other adverse health effects. Evidence mounted in the 1950s (Kluger, 1996).

In 1964, the first *Surgeon General's Report on Smoking and Health* was published. The report concluded that smoking was causally related to lung cancer, that it was the most important cause of chronic bronchitis, that it increased the risk of dying from chronic bronchitis and emphysema, and that it was related to coronary disease. Since then, reports by other Surgeons General have provided additional scientific and quantitative support for these conclusions and have focused on the particular need to reduce youth access to cigarettes. For example, a recent Surgeon General's report was devoted entirely to preventing tobacco use among young people (USDHHS, 1994).

The focus on teenagers is due, in part, to the fact that about one-half of adult smokers become regular smokers by age 18 (CDC, 1993a). In a summary of the Surgeon General's report, Elders et al. (1994) noted that nearly all first use of tobacco occurs prior to high school graduation. These authors also reported that the rate of increase in teenage smoking has not declined in the past few years, despite substantial declines in smoking in the population at large. A recent report (CDC, 1994) confirms that smoking among teenagers has actually increased during the past decade. One policy implication of these reports is that smoking morbidity and mortality can be reduced significantly if teenagers' access to cigarettes is limited (IOM, 1994).

The most recent scientific debate on smoking concerns the effects of passive smoking. In 1986, the Surgeon General reported a significant relationship between environmental tobacco smoke and lung cancer. In 1990, the Environmental Protection Agency (EPA) released a draft report that reviewed 24 epidemiological studies. The EPA concluded that ETS causes 3,800 lung cancer deaths each year (Altman, 1990), corroborating an earlier report on passive smoking from the Surgeon General (USDHHS, 1986).

Passive smoking appears to be a particular risk to infants and children. In a study on lung cancer and exposure to tobacco smoke in the household, Janerich and Thompson (1990) concluded that 17 percent of lung cancers among nonsmokers can be attributed to high levels of exposure during childhood and adolescence. Passive smoking has also been found to be a risk factor for other cancers. For example, a case-control study of women in Utah found that exposure to ETS three or more hours a day almost triples the risk of cervical cancer in nonsmoking women (Slattery et al., 1989).

The Political Evolution of Anti-Tobacco Legislation and Regulation

As the scientific evidence of tobacco's harmful effects mounted, legislative activity grew on both the state and federal levels. In states without laws preempting stronger local ordinances, municipalities have also been active in restricting public use of cigarettes.

Federal. Federal activity to regulate smoking has a mixed heritage. Along with providing subsidies for tobacco farmers, Congress has limited federal regulatory oversight and, in restricting smoking, has been largely stymied by tobacco industry lobbying pressure. At the same time, the emergence of the Surgeon General as a moral and scientific spokesman against smoking has added a significant federal voice to smoking reduction efforts.

In response to the 1964 Surgeon General's report on smoking, Congress enacted the Cigarette Labeling and Advertising Act in 1965, which required health warnings on all cigarette packages. The act superseded proposed Federal Trade Commission (FTC) rules requiring that manufacturers disclose on all packaging and advertisements that "cigarette smoking is dangerous to health" and "may cause death from cancer and other diseases." Instead, the act mandated the following warning on cigarette packaging: "Caution: Cigarette smoking may be hazardous to your health." Equally important, the act preempted states from imposing more stringent health warning requirements and prohibited federal agencies from requiring more stringent health warnings.

In 1967, the Federal Communications Commission (FCC) ruled that the "fairness doctrine" applied to cigarette commercials. As a result, all broadcasters who carried cigarette advertising were required to provide equal time to warn the public about cigarettes. In 1968, 1,300 anti-tobacco messages were aired by the three major networks (Lewit, Coate, and Grossman, 1981). A year later, Congress passed the Public Health Cigarette Smoking Act of 1969, banning all cigarette advertising from television and radio, eliminating the need for broadcasters to provide equal time for anti-tobacco messages. The ban was enacted with the acquiescence of the tobacco industry, which was beginning to be affected adversely by the anti-tobacco advertisements and feared greater regulatory activity (Kagan and Vogel,

1993). The act also amended the health warning on cigarettes to "Warning: The Surgeon General Has Determined That Cigarette Smoking Is Dangerous To Your Health." Additionally, Congress restricted the FTC from requiring manufacturers to include health warnings in print advertising and barred states from imposing "any requirement or prohibition based on smoking and health" on advertising and promotion of cigarettes packaged with labels conforming to the statute.

In 1972, the FTC and cigarette manufacturers agreed upon consent orders requiring all cigarette advertising to display the same warning required for cigarette packaging. Subsequently, the Comprehensive Smoking Education Act of 1984 (CSEA), required four rotating health warnings on all cigarette packages, and advertisements. More recently, the Comprehensive Smokeless Tobacco Health Education Act of 1986 required three rotating health warnings for all smokeless tobacco product packaging and advertising. In 1989, Congress voted to ban smoking on airline flights of less than two hours (later extended to flights under six hours).

In recent years, Congress has become more active in legislating tobacco controls in which children may be affected. Perhaps most significantly, the federal government enacted the 1992 Alcohol, Drug Abuse and Mental Health Agency Reorganization Act requiring states to enact and enforce laws against the sale and distribution of tobacco products to individuals under 18 years of age. Known as the Synar Amendment (42 USC 300x-26), the law conditions Alcohol, Drug Abuse, and Mental Health block grant allocations to the states on compliance with these provisions. If a state fails to enact or enforce such laws, its block grant allocations can be reduced by 10 percent in the first year, and up to 40 percent by the fourth year of noncompliance. The Synar Amendment took effect for all states in 1995. Congress also enacted the Pro Children Act of 1994, prohibiting smoking in indoor facilities that are routinely used for the delivery of certain services to children, including schools, libraries, and day care, health care, and early childhood development centers.

However, the tobacco industry continues to be a strong opponent, particularly on the federal regulatory level. To a large extent, the tobacco industry has successfully limited the extent of federal regulatory oversight. As Kluger (1996, p. 740) observes, it has been a "long-standing travesty that [has] allowed society's most dangerous consumer product to escape serious regulation." For example, the agency most likely to oversee tobacco products, the Food and Drug Administration (FDA), was effectively limited by congressional language in 1938 that failed to define tobacco as a food or drug that should be regulated (Kluger, 1996).

Since the 1960s, few federal agencies have attempted to promulgate tobacco use restrictions because of expected opposition from Congress or outright congressional prohibition of regulatory authority. Cigarettes have been specifically exempted from coverage under the Fair Labeling and Packaging Act of 1966, the Controlled Substances Act of 1970, the Consumer Product Safety Act of 1972 (establishing the Consumer Product Safety Commission), and the Toxic Substances Act of 1976. Other nonexempted regulatory agencies, including the EPA and the Occupational Safety and Health Administration (OSHA), have considered, but abandoned, efforts to regulate smoking. The EPA has determined that environmental tobacco smoke should be treated as a dangerous carcinogen but has yet to promulgate regulations that would implement this finding. Likewise, OSHA has proposed standards for regulating indoor air at private work sites, including restrictions on smoking, also without being able to implement the regulations.

In 1996, the FDA promulgated a series of regulations aimed at restricting youth access to tobacco. The FDA rule would ban cigarette sales in vending machines; ban tobacco billboard advertisements within 1,000 feet of schools or playgrounds; restrict ads in publications with more than 15 percent youth readership to black and white, text-only format; require the tobacco industry to fund a $150 million per year anti-tobacco media campaign; ban tobacco brand-name sponsorship of sporting events and concerts; and permit the FDA to regulate tobacco products.

Despite the relative absence of federal regulation of tobacco products, the importance of the reports of the Surgeons General on tobacco cannot be understated as a contributing factor in the emergence of a policy environment receptive to various tobacco control strategies (Jacobson, Wasserman, and Raube, 1993; Kagan and Vogel, 1993). As Kagan and Vogel (1993) point out, the authority of the Surgeon General's office and meticulous accumulation of scientific evidence have allowed the various Surgeons General to "advocate interventionist governmental policies." In particular, the 1986 Surgeon General's report on the dangers of environmental tobacco smoke undermined libertarian arguments that anti-tobacco laws were unnecessary to protect third parties from tobacco's harms and facilitated the expansion of state and local anti-tobacco laws (Jacobson, Wasserman, and Raube, 1993; Kagan and Skolnick, 1993).

State. Four trends capture state legislative developments since 1989: (1) the rise in the number of states enacting some smoking restrictions; (2) a legislative focus on enacting laws to restrict access to teenagers, including vending machine and point-of-sale restrictions; (3) the enactment of some form of nondiscrimination against smokers (30 states between 1989 and 1995, according to CSOH, 1995); and (4) the continued enactment of laws preempting stronger local ordinances (27 states according to CSOH, 1995; 17 according to CDC, 1995a). Taken at face value, these trends appear to be somewhat contradictory. In all likelihood, the legislative results represent the shifting balance between the tobacco industry and tobacco control proponents as various arguments, i.e., science versus individual freedoms, gain in the legislative debate. The trends also reflect the tradeoffs demanded as the price of legislation. For example, the only way to enact statewide clean indoor air act regulations in Florida and Illinois was to accede to preemption (Jacobson, Wasserman, and Raube, 1993).

The Legislative Debates. Most of the state legislative debates from the late 1970s through the mid- to late 1980s centered on the sufficiency of the scientific evidence to justify legislative intervention. When the debate was on the scientific evidence, the tobacco industry was on the defensive. Beginning in the mid- to late 1980s, there appeared to be a shift in the nature of the debate—away from science and toward consideration of personal freedom issues—largely resulting from the tobacco industry's strategy to emphasize individual rights (Jacobson, Wasserman, and Raube, 1993). This strategy met with some success, particularly in generating legislation to protect smokers from discrimination in employment, such as legislation enacted in Illinois, but was generally not sufficient to overcome the weight of the scientific evidence.

In the early to mid-1990s, the terms of the debate shifted once again, this time toward a focus on children. For many anti-tobacco advocates, the focus on children was likely to become an effective strategy because of its general political attractiveness to legislators and because it is difficult for the tobacco industry to publicly oppose restrictions on youth access. So far, largely to comply with the federal Synar Amendment, all states have enacted youth access restrictions. Even so, one prominent anti-tobacco activist recently objected to the youth access strategy as derogating from a more comprehensive attack on smoking (Glantz, 1996).

Restricting Smoking in Public Places. For the most part, statutes limiting smoking in public places were relatively rare prior to 1970. At that time, only 14 states[1] had laws that limited smoking. In 1977, 392 tobacco control bills were introduced in the various state legislatures, and 28 states enacted 44 bills into law (Christoffel and Stein, 1979). Although most of these bills involved matters such as taxation of cigarettes or control of transport, a considerable number sought to limit cigarette smoking in one way or another.

Today, 49 states restrict smoking in some manner in public places. These laws range from nominal restrictions, such as public buildings and schools in Indiana and Kentucky, to very extensive restrictions, such as prohibitions on smoking in many public places in Utah and Vermont. Only a few states have enacted comprehensive clean indoor air laws that restrict or prohibit smoking in a wide variety of public places. In addition, 43 states restrict smoking at public work sites, and 23 states restrict smoking in private work sites (CSOH, 1995). In Table 1.1, we combine 1995 published data from the Centers for Disease Control and the Coalition on Smoking OR Health to show state laws on several dimensions: clean indoor air regulations at government work sites, private work sites, and restaurants; youth access restrictions on vending machines and vendor licensing; advertising restrictions; and preemption and nondiscrimination provisions.

---

[1]For convenience, we include the District of Columbia as a state.

Table 1.1

Summary of State Laws by State and by Type of Restriction

	Smoke-Free Indoor Air			Youth Access to Tobacco Products			Preemption		Nondiscrimination
State	Gov't Work Sites	Private Work Sites	Restaurants	Vending Machine Restrictions	Licensing	Advertising Tobacco Products	CSOH	CDC	
AL					X				
AK	X	(a)	X	X	X				
AZ	X								X
AR	(a)			X	X				
CA	X	X	X	(a)		X	X	X	
CO	X			X					X
CT	X	X	X	X	X		X	X	X
DE	X	X	X		X		X	X	
FL	X	X	X	X	X		X	X	
GA				X	X				
HI	X		X	X					
ID	X		X	X					
IL	X	X	X	(a)		X	X	X	X
IN	X			X					X
IA	X	X	X	X	X		X	X	
KS	X		X		X				
KY	(a)			X	X	X	X	X	X
LA	X(b)	X(b)		X(b)	X	X	X	X	X
ME	X	X	X	X			X		X
MD	(a)	(a)	X	X	X				

Table 1.1—continued

State	Smoke-Free Indoor Air			Youth Access to Tobacco Products			Preemption		Nondiscrimination
	Gov't Work Sites	Private Work Sites	Restaurants	Vending Machine Restrictions	Licensing	Advertising Tobacco Products	CSOH	CDC	
MA	X		X	X	X		X		
MI	X		X	X	X	X	X	X	
MN	X	X	X	X					X
MS				X			X		X
MO	X	X	X	X					X
MT	X	X	X	X	X		X		X
NE	X(b)	X	X	X	X				
NV	X		X	X	X		X	X	X
NH	X	X	X	(a)	X				X
NJ	X	X		X	X		X		X
NM	X			X			X		X
NY	X	X	X	X	X		X		X
NC	(a)				X		X	X	X
ND	X		X		X				X
OH	X			X	X				
OK	X		X	X	X		X	X	X
OR	X		X	X			X		X
PA	X	X	X		X	X	X	X	
RI	X	X	X	(a)	X				X
SC	X				X			X	X
SD	X			X			X		X
TN				X			X	X	X
TX					X	X			

Table 1.1—continued

State	Smoke-Free Indoor Air			Youth Access to Tobacco Products			Preemption		Nondiscrimination
	Gov't Work Sites	Private Work Sites	Restaurants	Vending Machine Restrictions	Licensing	Advertising Tobacco Products	CSOH	CDC	
UT	X	X	X	X	X	X	X	X	
VT	X	X	X	X	X				
VA	X		X	X(b)			X	X	X
WA	X	(a)	X	X	X		X		
WA, DC	X	X	X	X	X				X
WV						X			X
WI	X	X	X	X	X		X		X
WY	X			X					X

SOURCES: Centers for Disease Control, 1995a; CSOH, 1995.

[a]CSOH, not CDC.

[b]CDC, not CSOH.

Two items stand out from Table 1.1. First, the sheer volume of tobacco control legislation suggests that tobacco remains a subject that legislators are willing to confront. Second, the tobacco industry has had considerable success at the state level in enacting legislation that preempts more-stringent local ordinances and prohibits discrimination against smokers, especially in employment. As many as 27 states have some form of preemptive legislation, often prohibiting local ordinances stronger than the provisions of state law (CSOH, 1995). As part of Washington State's youth access law, for example, the tobacco industry was able to include a provision that preempts local licensure or regulating tobacco sales in retail stores. Except for legislation in a few states, such as Minnesota, the tobacco industry has also been successful in preventing stringent clean indoor air regulations and in diluting enforcement authority.

Youth Access Restrictions. As of 1993, 47 states had enacted laws that prohibited the sale of tobacco products to persons under 18 years of age (Bierig, Weber, and Scarborough, 1994). By 1995, all states had restricted minors' access to tobacco products in one form or another. But as the IOM (1994) report on preventing nicotine addiction in children points out, these laws have gone largely unenforced since their enactment in the early part of the 20th century. "Despite increased national interest in curtailing underage smoking, minors still have virtually unimpeded access to tobacco products" (IOM, 1994, p. 201). Indeed, it was not until the late 1980s that public attention to youth access restrictions became an integral part of the policy agenda. Since then, local communities have shown a greater willingness to enact and enforce ordinances limiting minors' access to cigarettes.

Local. At the local level, the number of ordinances restricting smoking has also increased. In 1985, approximately 90 local communities restricted smoking in public places (CDC, 1989). By 1993, over 500 counties or cities had enacted anti-tobacco ordinances (CSOH, 1993; see also, Rigotti and Pashos, 1991). Currently, at least 782 communities have clean indoor air ordinances, 281 have enacted youth access ordinances, with 273 enacting both (Americans for Nonsmokers Rights, 1996). Further growth in local ordinances restricting smoking behavior is limited by statewide laws preempting local ordinances and laws that protect smokers from discrimination for smoking behavior.

A growing number of local anti-tobacco laws have targeted teenagers' tobacco use. For example, according to the Surgeon General's report on preventing tobacco use among young people, at least 30 cities in Minnesota, New York, California, Maryland, New Jersey, and Louisiana have outlawed the use of cigarette vending machines. Moreover, many other cities have adopted laws that limit teenage access to cigarette vending machines by requiring that such machines be placed in view of an employee, restricting the use of the machines to certain types of businesses and/or private facilities, or requiring the use of locking devices on the machines (USDHHS, 1994; IOM, 1994).

For a variety of reasons, including more-stringent regulation of vending machines, minors now purchase most cigarettes at convenience stores and gas stations. Thus, local ordinances permitting license removal from vendors who sell cigarettes to minors is a more powerful law than laws requiring cigarettes to be sold from behind the counter.

In addition to federal advertising regulations, several localities have restricted advertising for tobacco products. For example, Boston and San Francisco, along with many other cities, have banned tobacco advertising in their mass transit systems (Bierig, Weber, and Scarborough, 1994). In 1994, Baltimore banned publicly visible cigarette and alcohol billboards, with some minor exceptions (Garner, 1996). Cincinnati has also prohibited cigarette advertisements near schools, playgrounds, and parks. Although, as Garner (1996) recounts, Baltimore's ad ban was recently upheld by the Fourth Circuit Court of Appeals,[2] a recent U.S. Supreme Court case overturned restrictions on alcohol advertising based on First Amendment commercial speech freedom, casting doubt on the courts' willingness to uphold all but the most narrowly tailored advertising restrictions.

Judicial Involvement. Until recently, courts have played a decidedly secondary role in regulating tobacco products, generally permitting

---

[2] *Penn Advertising of Baltimore, Inc. v. Mayor of Baltimore*, 63 F.3d 1318 (4th Cir. 1995).

states and localities wide ranging authority to regulate tobacco products. The courts' reluctance to overturn laws regulating smoking was succinctly summarized by the U.S. Supreme Court in *Austin v. Tennessee,* 179 U.S., p. 343 (1900), in holding that the regulation of cigarette sales was within the powers of the states:

> Without undertaking to affirm or deny their evil effects, we think it within the province of the legislature to say how far [cigarettes] may be sold or to prohibit their sale entirely and there is no reason to doubt that the act in question is designed for the protection of the public health (179 U.S., pp. 348–349).

Aside from the uncertainty noted earlier about the courts' willingness to scrutinize commercial speech (that is, tobacco advertisements), it seems unlikely that courts would intervene to block tobacco control regulations. Indeed, the Florida Supreme Court recently upheld a local ordinance that required applicants for public employment in North Miami to refrain from smoking for one year prior to their application (*City of North Miami v. Kurtz,* 1995 Lexis 568 (Fla. 1995)). Likewise, courts have upheld total bans on vending machines as a means of restricting youth access to cigarettes (Bierig, Weber, and Scarborough, 1994).

As a result, there have actually been only a few challenges to state or local tobacco control laws. However, juries have been reluctant to hold cigarette manufacturers responsible for the free choices an adult smoker makes, and courts have not imposed strict liability on the manufacturers, thus limiting the incidence of litigation (see, e.g., Schwartz, 1993). The tobacco industry's defense that the smoker assumes the risk has meant that "tort liability has contributed virtually nothing to the array of strategies employed to control tobacco use" (Rabin, 1991, p. 494).[3]

Effectiveness of Regulations Limiting Smoking Behavior. The literature on the effectiveness of clean indoor air regulations demonstrates the inherent conundrum underlying these laws. To be effective, some continuing enforcement presence is needed, but most

---

[3]As many have noted, there is a certain irony in the way that the health warnings from the 1960s, enacted over tobacco industry opposition, have virtually insulated the industry from tort liability.

clean indoor air laws lack a strong enforcement component and are perceived to be self-enforcing. If, in fact, they are not self-enforcing, the laws are unlikely to be particularly effective.

For example, Rigotti et al. (1988, 1992, 1993, 1994) have conducted a significant amount of research regarding the compliance of businesses with anti-tobacco laws, in particular the self-enforcement approach. Results from these studies, conducted in Cambridge, Massachusetts, indicate that awareness of the local no-smoking ordinance in workplaces declined from 92 percent to 73 percent over the two years after passage. Eighty percent of companies surveyed restricted smoking 3 and 24 months after passage, but only half the businesses fully complied with the law at either date. Based on this work, Rigotti, Stoto, and Schelling (1994) conclude that business size is important in determining compliance, with small businesses less likely to comply; that the anti-tobacco laws led to a high level of smoking restrictions; and that reminders to business are needed to avoid erosion in compliance over time.[4]

Effectiveness of Regulations Restricting Minors' Access to Tobacco Products. Several studies have shown how easily minors can purchase cigarettes (see, e.g., DiFranza and Brown, 1992; Radecki and Zdunich, 1993; DiFranza, Savageau, and Aisquith, 1996). The literature on enforcement of youth access restrictions is less extensive but demonstrates generally the need to enforce these laws. Unlike the clean indoor air regulations, youth access restrictions are not susceptible to self-enforcement, largely because there are strong economic incentives associated with completing the transaction.

For example, Feighery, Altman, and Shaffer (1991) examined the effects of combined community education and enforcement efforts in four Northern California communities. They found that the combined enforcement and education approach resulted in reduced tobacco sales to minors, but that education efforts alone had only a limited effect. Similarly, Jason et al. (1991) examined the enforcement of laws against selling cigarettes to minors. They found that aggressive enforcement and follow-up compliance checks led to 96

---

[4]For similar conclusions in other settings and areas, see, Nordstrom and DeStefano (1995); Lewit, Botsko, and Shapiro (1993); Patten et al. (1995); and Brownson et al. (1995).

percent compliance by cigarette vendors against sales to minors, and a substantial reduction (50 percent) in tobacco use among local junior high school students.

As a follow-up to the 1991 study, Jason et al. (1996) studied the accessibility of cigarettes to "older" minors. The ability of minors aged 15 through 17 to purchase cigarettes from merchants in Woodridge, Illinois, was compared with the ability of minors aged 13 and 14. The results from 16 compliance checks revealed that sales rates to the 13- and 14-year-olds were below 13 percent. Sales rates to the 15- and 16-year-olds were below 20 percent, while sales rates to the 17-year-olds were 25 percent. Based on these results, the authors suggest that interventions designed to restrict minors' access to cigarettes must address the differing abilities of minors of differing ages to purchase cigarettes.

RESEARCH QUESTIONS

The Policy Context

According to a former Surgeon General, cigarette smoking is the single most important preventable cause of death in our society (USDHHS, 1982; CDC, 1989). Each year, approximately 420,000 Americans die due to tobacco use—eight times the number who lost their lives during 10 years of fighting in the Vietnam War. Cigarette smoking is responsible for one in six American deaths each year: 30 percent of all cancer deaths, 21 percent of deaths from coronary heart disease, 18 percent of deaths from stroke, and 82 percent of deaths from chronic obstructive pulmonary disease (CDC, 1993a; McGinnis and Foege, 1993).

Although smoking prevalence among men has fallen from over 50 percent in 1965 to close to 25 percent in 1993, 46 million adults and 3 million teenagers still smoke (NCI, 1993). Another report (CDC, 1996) confirms that smoking among teenagers has increased from 27.5 percent in 1991, to 30 percent in 1993, and to 34.8 percent in 1995. More than 75 percent of those underage smokers indicated that they had not been asked to provide identification prior to purchasing cigarettes. The policy implication is that smoking morbidity and mortality can be reduced significantly if teenagers' access to cigarettes is limited.

In response, a growing number of state and local anti-tobacco laws have targeted teenagers by, for instance, prohibiting or limiting the use of cigarette vending machines. And the federal government has enacted the Synar Amendment, discussed above, which requires states to enact and enforce laws against the sale and distribution of tobacco products to individuals under 18 years of age. Although only a few studies have addressed the implementation and enforcement of state and local anti-tobacco laws (Burns et al., 1992), previous research suggests that tobacco sales to minors can be reduced by enforcing age restriction laws (Feighery, Altman, and Shaffer, 1991; Jason et al. 1991, 1996).

Research Questions

In light of the above, our study was designed to address the following research questions:

- How are anti-tobacco laws—both clean indoor air provisions and youth access restrictions—implemented and enforced at both the state and local levels?
- What is the effect of strong statewide anti-tobacco legislation on the development and implementation of local anti-tobacco ordinances?
- What role does an anti-tobacco coalition play once statewide legislation is enacted?
- What strategy has the tobacco industry adopted in response to the implementation and enforcement of anti-tobacco laws?
- What are the most effective legislative/regulatory/policy strategies given the results of this study?

We also address the following specific issues: the process by which anti-tobacco laws and ordinances are diffused throughout the community; the effects of such laws in the absence of a strong enforcement mechanism; the relationship between statewide laws and local ordinances; the relative effectiveness of various legislative provisions, especially those limiting teenage access to cigarettes; the role of anti-tobacco coalitions in seeing that laws enacted are adequately enforced; whether these laws are merely symbolic legislative statements as opposed to meaningful policy options for reducing teenage smoking initiation rates and cigarette consumption; the barriers to effective diffusion; the process of diffusing anti-tobacco restrictions across communities within a state; and how information about anti-tobacco restrictions is disseminated to the public.

CONCEPTUAL APPROACH AND HYPOTHESES

At the heart of our conceptual approach are three complementary theses, based on our previous research and review of the literature, about the legislative and implementation processes. The first concept is that it is easier for anti-tobacco advocates to organize around the enactment of legislation than it is to sustain the momentum to monitor the implementation and enforcement of anti-tobacco laws. The legislative process has a shorter time frame and a tangible outcome, while the implementation process requires a very focused and sustained effort. However, the tobacco industry is as motivated to undermine implementation as it is to oppose legislated smoking restrictions in the first place. We hypothesize that anti-tobacco coalitions will not be organized around enforcement and implementation issues; instead, their primary focus will remain on enacting legislation.

The second concept is that absent a strong enforcement mechanism, statewide anti-tobacco legislation may represent a mere symbolic statement about the state's desire to control smoking that is dependent on people's good will for success. If so, local ordinances with local implementation may be more effective in reducing smoking in public places and in curtailing teenage cigarette consumption than statewide legislation. Thus, we hypothesize that local entities will be more aggressive in enforcement activities than state officials. We also hypothesize that states and localities will not aggressively enforce clean indoor air regulations but will aggressively enforce youth access restrictions.

The third concept is that efforts by state and local anti-tobacco coalitions will be integral to successful enforcement and implementation of any anti-tobacco laws. Absent a viable and motivated coalition to impel official enforcement and business compliance with smoking restrictions, enforcement and implementation will lag. In our previous work, we speculated that many anti-tobacco regulations would be self-enforcing, given the unlikelihood of stringent enforcement. This study provided an opportunity to examine that hypothesis at both the state and local levels.

Our conceptual approach is informed by the large body of research on program implementation that has emerged during the past two decades. Two key principles from the implementation literature are important for this study. First, implementation policy cannot be separated from other aspects of policy development and formulation, including the legislative process. Second, program implementation is a political process involving various interest groups and a wide range of stakeholders, not just governmental officials (Palumbo and Calista, 1990; Kingdon, 1984).

As a result, the implementation and enforcement of tobacco control laws are likely to be as much a function of political pressure as the enactment of legislation. An effective implementation process is integral to and a critical aspect of successful policymaking (Palumbo and Calista, 1990). Program objectives are likely to be interpreted differently by various levels of government during the implementation process (Pressman and Wildavsky, 1976). In tobacco control implementation, state officials may have very different interests at stake than local officials.

Other researchers note that an effective implementation process will be structured around pressure and support (Zellman, 1994). Pressure focuses attention on the new policy and increases the likelihood of compliance. Mazmanian and Sabatier (1983) note the importance of committed implementors as the key to achieving policy goals. Support may include adequate financial resources, a system of rewards that recognizes compliance efforts, and room for bottom-level input into the process (McLaughlin, 1987). In addition, stakeholders decide whether to comply by calculating two kinds of costs: (1) the likelihood the mandate will be strictly enforced and compliance failures will be detected and (2) the severity of sanctions for noncompliance. If enforcement is strict and the sanction costs are high, compliance is more likely (McDonnell and Elmore, 1987).

One theoretical model posits that four key factors determine implementation outcomes: the policy formation process prior to the law being implemented, organizational and interorganizational behavior, bureaucratic activity, and the response by target groups (Winter, 1990; Mazmanian and Sabatier, 1983; Goggin, 1987; Zellman, 1994). We considered the first variable in our previous research (Jacobson, Wasserman, and Raube, 1993). This report focuses on the remaining three variables.

ORGANIZATION OF THE REPORT

The report is organized as follows. In the next chapter, we set forth the case study methods plus brief synopses of the case studies. The full case study for each state can be found in Appendixes A through G. We then report our results, organized around cross-cutting themes synthesized from the state-specific case studies. In the final chapter, we discuss our results and identify some of the policy implications of our research, with regard to both tobacco control and other public health measures.

Chapter Two

OVERVIEW OF THE CASE STUDIES

CASE STUDY METHODS

Site Selection

Although it would have been desirable to review state laws and local ordinances in every state, resource constraints prevented such an ambitious agenda. Instead, we limited our case study sites to seven states: California, Arizona, Texas, New York, Minnesota, Illinois, and Florida. These include the six states from our previous study of the political evolution of anti-tobacco legislation (Jacobson, Wasserman, and Raube, 1993) plus California. As shown in Table 2.1, these states represent a mix of legal environments across several dimensions. Some have strong statewide legislation and weak local ordinances (Minnesota), others have the reverse (Texas), and one has strong statewide and local anti-tobacco laws (New York). The states also vary in their approaches to vending machine and sample distribution restrictions.

We chose to revisit the states in our earlier study for several reasons. First, they vary across dimensions of interest to policymakers. For instance, the states vary in the locus of enforcement responsibility, the strength of legislative enforcement provisions, and the extent to which smoking in public places is regulated by state and local laws. Also, revisiting Illinois and Florida, states with controversial preemption provisions, enables us to assess how preemption affects anti-tobacco coalition operations and local enforcement and implementation efforts. Second, we had established contacts that

Table 2.1

Legal Environment of Proposed Sites

State	Restrictions on Smoking in Public Places		Vending Machine Restrictions	Sample Distribution Restrictions
	State	Local		
AZ	None	Minimal	None	None
CA	Strong	Strong	None	Ban
FL	Moderate	Preempted	Placement restrictions	Minors
IL	Moderate	Preempted	Sign posting	Minors
MN	Strong	Moderate	Placement restrictions	Ban
NY	Strong	Strong	Placement restrictions	Restricted
TX	None	Moderate	Sign posting	None

would facilitate data collection. Third, we would be able to assess changes over time in coalition activity.

In Illinois, the statewide legislation does not include any specific enforcement provisions, but both the New York and Minnesota legislation include strong enforcement provisions. In California, there is recent strong statewide legislation, but many communities have more stringent anti-tobacco ordinances, raising questions as to how such communities will react to the new statewide tobacco controls. We intentionally excluded tobacco-producing states from consideration because these jurisdictions have few state or local anti-tobacco restrictions in place.

Each site was visited once, for a total of five days per site. To ensure consistency of interview results across sites, we developed an interview guide (described below) and conducted the first site interview jointly. Within each state, we conducted a state-level analysis that involved reinterviewing many of the people we interviewed in our previous study. In addition, we visited local sites within each state, as shown in Table 2.2. Selection criteria for the local sites included community size, geographic location, type and strength of the ordinances, and duration of the ordinances. We visited a mix of small and large municipalities. Before selecting the local municipalities, we discussed our selection criteria with our contacts in each state. In

Table 2.2

State and Local Sites Included in Analysis

State	Local Sites
Arizona	Cottonwood
	Flagstaff
	Scottsdale
	Tempe
California	Contra Costa County
	Los Angeles
Florida	Tampa
	Miami
	Tallahassee
Illinois	Chicago
	Woodridge
Minnesota	Roseville
	Shoreview
New York	New York City
	Nassau County
	Suffolk County
	Chatauqua County
Texas	Arlington
	Austin

making the final selection, we chose sites that had experience with enforcement and implementation activity.

Data Collection

Interview Protocol. Before conducting the site visits, we developed a semi-structured interview protocol, attached as Appendix H. The protocol was designed to elicit discussion about the following specific topics: (1) recent or current tobacco control initiatives; (2) implementation and enforcement strategies, along with changes in strategies over time; (3) stakeholder roles in enforcement and implementation; (4) the relationship between statewide anti-tobacco legislation and local ordinances; (5) how anti-tobacco coalitions organize and operate to facilitate implementation and enforcement; and (6) barriers to effective enforcement, including tobacco industry responses to enforcement and implementation efforts.

Interview Targets. In each state, we interviewed local and state enforcement agency officials and representatives of affected businesses (and their associations), such as restaurants, convenience stores, and other cigarette vendors. We met with leaders of anti-tobacco advocacy groups, voluntary health organizations (such as the American Cancer Society, the American Lung Association, and the American Heart Association), and, where possible, with officials and attorneys for the tobacco industry. The interview targets were selected based on discussions with our contacts in each state and based on the need to provide specific information about the implementation and enforcement process. In addition, we used a triangulation strategy to obtain information about the same questions from different respondents where possible. In all, we interviewed 137 individuals across the seven study states.

Most of the respondents represented either state and local enforcement agencies or anti-tobacco coalition members. As expected, tobacco industry representatives were not eager to participate in this study. However, we were able to interview representatives of other affected industries, such as restaurant associations.

Documentary Evidence. We collected all available data on enforcement and implementation at both the state and local levels. For example, we secured records from local enforcement agencies (usually either the county health department or the police department) on the number of warnings and citations issued, complaints received, reports of violations, the distribution of offenses, recidivism rates, and sanctions imposed. We examined similar records maintained by state departments of health or other state enforcement agencies. We also attempted to obtain any studies conducted showing the costs and benefits of anti-tobacco laws or enforcement activity.

Some state-level data were available as a result of the Synar Amendment. The amendment (see 42 USC 300x-26(b)(1)) requires states to submit annual reports, beginning in 1994 for most states, describing their enforcement activities, extent of success in reducing tobacco availability to teenagers, and strategies for enforcement. Because many state Synar programs are just getting started, there is considerable variation in state-level data quality, in terms of both accuracy and comprehensiveness.

Data Analysis. The analysis focuses on synthesizing the results of our document reviews and interviews and on extracting a set of cross-cutting themes, or lessons, that can be applied by legislators, other policymakers, and anti-tobacco advocates. The primary form of analysis is descriptive, comparing and contrasting information across sites along several dimensions of interest. These dimensions include degrees of enforcement at the state and local levels; the process by which tobacco control initiatives are diffused to the public; the role of interest groups, specifically anti-tobacco coalitions and the tobacco industry; and barriers to effective implementation and enforcement.

To the extent possible, interview transcripts captured participants' verbatim responses. Based on the interview notes, we prepared separate case studies for each of the sites visited. We then analyzed all of the case studies for common themes and differences across the sites. Next, the case studies were sent to at least one of the respondents at each site for technical review. Comments received from the reviewers were incorporated into the case studies. Finally, we collaborated closely with one another throughout the analysis to ensure consistency in analyzing site-specific results.

Study Limitations

As with any methodological approach, qualitative research methods have certain inherent limitations. These methods are not designed to test hypotheses or to be generalizable beyond the population from which the sample is drawn. Specifically, resource constraints limited the number of interviews that could be conducted in any one site. While we believe that we have interviewed a diverse sample of stakeholders at each site, we were not able to meet with as many respondents as we initially identified. In particular, representatives of the tobacco industry were generally not willing to participate in this study. Also, the documentary evidence of enforcement activity varies considerably across our sites, making comparisons difficult.

SYNOPSES OF CASE STUDIES

In this section, we present synopses of each case study. Our full case studies can be found in Appendixes A through G.

Texas

Historically, the anti-tobacco forces in Texas have been unsuccessful in passing significant statewide tobacco control legislation—both with respect to clean indoor air and teen access—at the state level. To a large extent, the failure to enact such legislation stems from the success of the tobacco industry in creating roadblocks in the state's House of Representatives as well as to a general antipathy toward passing legislation that is viewed by many as an attempt to regulate personal behavior (Jacobson et al., 1993). In fact, according to several observers, a series of repeated setbacks in the state legislature has led anti-tobacco activists to virtually abandon their efforts to pass a statewide clean indoor air bill and instead to focus on ensuring that the tobacco industry fails to have legislation enacted that would preempt local tobacco control initiatives.

The failure to enact a statewide tobacco control bill has left many proponents of tougher smoking laws with a deep sense of cynicism. One observer noted that

> you have to be very suspicious of any [tobacco control] law that's passed on the state level. Many of us would give up trying to pass a meaningful statewide law if we could be guaranteed that the legislature would never pass a preemption bill.

At the same time, the series of successive losses at the state level has caused the anti-tobacco coalition to change its overall strategy. An integral component of this new strategy is encouraging local communities to pass ordinances aimed at both restricting smoking in public places and limiting teenagers' access to cigarettes.

Texas has witnessed the passage of anti-tobacco ordinances in nearly half of the state's 200 largest cities (Texas Department of Health, 1991). As one observer pointed out, "Texas has been relatively successful at picking away at the problem on the local level." To gain insight into how local ordinances have been implemented and enforced, we conducted site visits to two Texas cities that have recently enacted anti-tobacco ordinances: Austin and Arlington.

The absence of significant tobacco control legislation at the state level—save a prohibition on the sale of cigarettes to minors—leaves issues related to the state's role in implementation and enforcement to be of little more than academic interest. While the state has made some effort to comply with the requirements of the Synar Amendment to preserve its alcohol and drug abuse block grants, no state-level tobacco control initiative is, or has been, in the offing.

At the same time, staff from the Texas Department of Health and other state-level organizations have actively supported local initiatives both to restrict teen access to cigarettes and to limit smoking in public places. Over the last decade, many locales have successfully enacted ordinances in both of these areas, but implementation and enforcement efforts have met with more mixed success.

We observed, for instance, that the Austin restaurant ordinance has proven somewhat problematic. Because no formal compliance studies have been undertaken, we are unable to report the precise extent to which affected businesses obey the law. Although anecdotal evidence indicates that compliance is generally high, instances of noncompliance abound, and almost all observers agree that the law has gaping holes. Moreover, disgruntled merchants are willing to risk being cited for noncompliance, knowing that it is unlikely that a court action will actually be brought against them.

However, the case of Arlington illustrates that it is possible to successfully enact, implement, and enforce a rather stringent local ordinance, which was ultimately found to enjoy broad public support, even among some of its initial opponents. A number of interviewees attributed the ordinance's success to the incrementalist approach adopted by the city council, the fact that there were a number of city council people around to "carry the torch," the public's solid support for additional controls, and the intelligence of spokespeople on both sides of the issue.

The main enforcement barrier in both of these communities appears to be resource constraints. As a result, enforcement is largely complaint-driven, and no systematic inspections are carried out, for instance, by code officers. Even in the absence of resource constraints, however, it is difficult to imagine that it would be cost-beneficial to conduct a rigorous series of inspections on a regular basis. For one thing, compliance with the ordinances in the two cities is generally felt to be quite high, although more so in Arlington than in Austin. Second, and perhaps more important, it is likely that stringent enforcement efforts may provoke a backlash at the state level. That is, if the tobacco industry's fabricated image of a "smoking police" is in some sense realized, then passage of a state bill that preempts local ordinances seems all the more likely. As one interviewee summed it up, "if you get greedy, you'll lose."

Arizona

Tobacco control, as practiced in Arizona, is primarily a local affair. Despite repeated attempts on the part of anti-tobacco advocates and the state's tobacco control coalition, the state has failed to enact any stringent tobacco control laws. That is, while the state prohibits the sale of cigarettes to minors, it regulates smoking in only a handful of public places such as elevators, buses, schools, and health care institutions. Moreover, in the view of many observers, the prospects for passing a significant statewide bill remain bleak.

Nevertheless, for a number of reasons, the case of Arizona remains an interesting one from a tobacco-control perspective. First, the state's coalition, which was filled with internal strife only a few short years ago, played an instrumental role in passing a 1994 ballot initiative that raised the state's cigarette excise tax by 40 cents per pack. Second, the state continues to provide striking examples of how local communities can enact and implement a broad array of tobacco control measures. And third, through its Synar Amendment–related activities and other initiatives, the state has generated quantitative data on several key tobacco control issues.

The Arizona Department of Health Services' response to Synar was to initiate a set of pilot projects throughout the state aimed at reducing youth access. Through a competitive bidding process, the department selected three cities (Tempe, Flagstaff, and Tucson) to receive awards of approximately $30,000 each.

The pilot project's results were mixed. As shown in Table 2.3, two of the three sites, Tempe and Flagstaff, achieved significant reductions in the rate of illegal sales to minors between the baseline "sting" operation and the second follow-up. (In the case of Flagstaff, the lowest illegal sales rate was actually observed during the first follow-up.) Note that while the rate of illegal sales in Tucson increased over the baseline—which was quite low in comparison to the other

Table 2.3

Rate of Illegal Sales of Tobacco to Minors in Arizona Cities

Community	Baseline	First Follow-up	Second Follow-up
Flagstaff	.62	.24	.32
Tempe	.65	.62	.27
Tucson	.28	.37	.30

SOURCE: Arizona Department of Health Services, 1995.

sites—in each of the two follow-up years, the final illegal sales rate for that city was comparable to that of the other two cities.

With respect to changes in the prevalence of teenage smoking, the results were not encouraging. As shown in Table 2.4, although the prevalence of smoking among 10th graders in Flagstaff declined by two percentage points after initiation of the intervention, the corresponding rates for Tempe and Tucson increased by two percentage points and five percentage points, respectively.

Taken together, the two tables illustrate an important point: Demonstrated reductions in illegal sales rates to minors may not affect minors' cigarette consumption. Take, for example, the case of Tempe. Although the illegal sales rate dropped dramatically in that city between the baseline inspection and the second follow-up, the prevalence rate increased by two percentage points. One possible explanation for these seemingly inconsistent results is simply that the inspections served to concentrate sales to minors in a smaller number of stores willingly to sell cigarettes to minors. Alternatively,

Table 2.4

Smoking Prevalence Rates Among 10th Graders in Arizona Cities (in percentage)

	Flagstaff	Tempe	Tucson
Pre-intervention	41	24	20
Post-intervention	39	26	25

SOURCE: Arizona Department of Health Services, 1995.

minors in Tempe may simply choose to buy cigarettes in a neighboring city, such as Mesa or Phoenix, that has not yet cracked down on vendors.

Arizona's experiences with tobacco control laws have produced their share of successes and failures. For example, as noted, the state's approach for complying with the requirements of the Synar Amendment, at least initially, produced mixed, if not somewhat discouraging, results. And while the City of Tempe's vending machine ordinance was all but ignored by vendors, a number of the local ordinances passed should be considered resounding successes from a tobacco control perspective, including the Flagstaff restaurant ordinance and the Scottsdale vending machine ban. Despite differences in the success of these laws, the sites studied showed some remarkable consistencies with respect to roles that some of the key stakeholders played in the implementation and enforcement process.

For example, at both the state and local levels, we found that while a myriad of organizations played important roles in enacting tobacco control laws, government agencies played the central, if not the exclusive, role in implementation and enforcement efforts. One member of the statewide tobacco control coalition put it succinctly, saying that "the main mission of the coalition is enactment."

Additionally, we found that the tobacco industry's representatives confined their most strenuous opposition efforts to the state level, where they made repeated attempts to have preemption legislation introduced. Interestingly, while they maintained at least some presence in each of the locales studied, they conducted themselves, for the most part, in a rather low-key manner, limiting the bulk of their activities during the enactment phase of the process to providing financial support to front groups (e.g., restaurant and merchant associations that virtually sprung up overnight once an ordinance was introduced) and writing periodic letters to the editors of local newspapers complaining about the ordinances' burdens as they perceived them.

Minnesota

With over 20 years of experience with tobacco control legislation, Minnesota represents a fertile site for study. In a sense, the state provides an opportunity for examining the long-term consequences of an organized tobacco control movement. In short, the state is a "mature market" with respect to tobacco control laws.

Perhaps one of the most interesting aspects of the Minnesota case study is the evolving nature of the roles played by various stakeholders. There are currently several factions that play major roles in the state's tobacco control efforts, including the Smokefree 2000 Coalition, the Association for Nonsmokers—Minnesota (ANSR), and the staff from Project ASSIST. These factions appear to both compete and cooperate with one another. Additionally, the influence of Minnesota's Department of Human Services has begun to be felt in connection with its Synar-related activities. Still, this agency remains very much a secondary player, and one that is viewed by many as having no genuine interest in tobacco control but is simply out to preserve its block grant funds.

The Smokefree 2000 Coalition has mostly concerned itself with issues related to enacting new statewide legislation and preserving the progress that has already been achieved (i.e., fighting the tobacco industry's preemption efforts). Its present focus is on passing a statewide youth access law. Toward that end, it has recently devoted itself to supporting local ordinance development, reasoning that such ordinances are a necessary precursor to a statewide bill and that the greater the number of local ordinances, the greater the likelihood that a state bill will be passed that does not contain a preemption provision.

ANSR has played a critical role in both the development of local ordinances and in their implementation and enforcement. ANSR's efforts have received almost universally positive reviews. A large number of interviewees indicated that ANSR, as opposed to the Smokefree 2000 Coalition, provides the bulk of the leadership on smoking issues and that it has a powerful influence on both state and local officials. Additionally, it has been very active at the local level and has developed a sophisticated ordinance diffusion strategy, which involves everything from selecting target communities that are adjacent to communities that have recently passed ordinances to providing technical assistance to communities and organizing large-scale compliance checks.

For several years now, the Minnesota Department of Health has maintained an uneasy relationship with tobacco control advocates throughout the state. While many people give this department credit for obtaining, and subsequently administering, the ASSIST grant, the department has come under fire for being all but mute on tobacco control issues. In the words of one respondent, "The department has not had a direct voice in tobacco control." As a result, the department has been essentially marginalized by the state's tobacco control community, which instead has looked to the Minnesota Attorney General's Office (which is headed by a Democrat who is often at odds with the state's Republican governor) for leadership.

The tobacco industry maintains a formidable presence in Minnesota, as elsewhere. To a great extent, however, it limits its activities to the state level, where it has been successful in turning back major attempts to amend the state's Clean Indoor Air Act as well as blocking efforts to pass a teen access law that does not preempt local ordinances. The strength of the industry's influence at the state level has transformed the strategy adopted by tobacco control proponents to a focus on the local level. As one such individual stated, "Until recently, I felt it would be easy to do things on the state level, but I now believe that you have to do things at the local level because the industry isn't there." That sentiment was echoed by a former city councilman who noted that "the advantage of the local level is that [the tobacco industry] can't get to you because the campaigns don't require large amounts of money."

The interviewees identified three major barriers to more-effective implementation and enforcement of tobacco control laws. The first was simply that, for reasons that remain largely inexplicable in light of the toll taken by tobacco on morbidity and mortality, the smoking issue lacked the salience that is accorded other issues. As one interviewee bluntly put it, "Smoking is not handguns. As a result, it is often difficult to mobilize people to action." A second respondent indicated that "people don't see tobacco as a threat because they don't see the consequences immediately." And a third said simply that "tobacco control is not a priority for most people."

Related to this is the concern that even anti-tobacco activists in the state appear to focus their attention on enacting new statewide laws and local ordinances rather than on implementation and enforcement issues. One long-time activist in the state lamented that "implementation and enforcement are our weakest points. Nobody is monitoring in a systematic way how the laws we pass are implemented and enforced."

A second barrier revolves around the notion of what many interviewees referred to as "institutionalization," which is essentially the process through which tobacco enforcement becomes part of the general fabric of local law enforcement. There was virtually unanimous agreement on the part of the respondents that regular compliance checks were essential to ensure that vendors refrain from selling cigarettes to minors. At the same time, many individuals expressed concern that such checks would not be carried out in the absence of ongoing financial support. In some communities, such as Shoreview, license fees make the system financially self-sufficient, but even in those instances there is no assurance that the local police department will conduct checks on a regular basis.

Third, while not technically an implementation or enforcement barrier, the fact that the state has been successful in passing a wide-ranging clean indoor air law may have impeded progress in this area at the local level, since communities may believe that clean indoor air ordinances are superfluous in light of the state law. Yet in the minds of many anti-tobacco advocates nothing could be further from the truth because the state law fails to prohibit smoking in a large number of public places and it provides no guarantees to nonsmokers that they will be able to enjoy smoke-free air when frequenting public places.

Minnesota's long history with smoking regulation has generated some important insights into the relationship between state and local tobacco control regulations. One observer of tobacco control regulation in Minnesota has characterized the relationship as a "leapfrog effect," referring to the phenomenon that activity at one level serves as a catalyst for activity at another. For instance, the 1975 passage of the state's Clean Indoor Air Act "built a culture or tone of acceptability" for tobacco control. This, in turn, made it possible for local communities to pass tobacco control ordinances.

And now the large number of local ordinances will potentially provide the groundwork for passing a statewide teen access law.

It should also be noted that there appears to be a second dimension to this effect, and that is the apparent tendency for local communities to attempt to one-up each other. According to one interviewee, local communities "are willing to go one better than their neighbors and no further." This is perhaps the heart of the diffusion process. That is, it is unrealistic to expect communities to adopt restrictive anti-tobacco laws in a vacuum. Each law must build upon what has been previously accomplished in a given community and in neighboring ones. Clearly, an initial spark is required—in fact, one councilman described his city's ordinance as "spreading like wildfire" once it was passed—but then the process quickly becomes an incremental one in which city council members are almost literally looking over the shoulders of their counterparts in other communities.

California

Since the passage of Proposition 99 in 1988—which increased California's cigarette excise tax by 25 cents per pack and used the proceeds to finance tobacco-related education and research programs, media campaigns, and health services—California has been in the forefront of the tobacco control movement. A number of significant anti-tobacco laws have been enacted at the state level over the last eight years, which attempt to control teen access to cigarettes and to place restrictions on smoking in public places. In addition, nearly 300 of the state's 468 cities have passed local ordinances to control smoking in public places, including workplaces, and 152 of those cities have passed ordinances that prohibit smoking in all workplaces (Ellis, Hobart, and Reed, 1995).

Apart from Proposition 99, two significant pieces of tobacco control legislation passed the California State Legislature in recent years. The first is the Stop Tobacco Access to Kids Enforcement Act, which, as the name implies, was enacted in an effort to reduce teenagers' access to cigarettes, and the second is Assembly Bill 13 (AB-13), which bans smoking in most workplaces.

The California Department of Health Services' Tobacco Control Section serves as the key agency for coordinating the state's tobacco control initiatives. A number of interviewees suggested that the department is focused on what they refer to as the "denormalization" of tobacco use, which essentially involves changing community norms (largely through public education campaigns) to reflect the notion that tobacco use is socially unacceptable in many different ways, including exposing individuals to environmental tobacco smoke and selling cigarettes and other tobacco products to minors. The denormalization strategy is, in effect, an attempt to marginalize smokers. The concept of denormalization was developed, in part, to contrast sharply with the tobacco industry's notion of "accommodation."

In the minds of some observers, the large number of local ordinances that were passed by cities and counties throughout California appears to have created a climate of acceptability for statewide controls. Additionally, the recent defeat of Proposition 188—a tobacco industry–sponsored initiative that would have preempted local ordinances restricting smoking in public places in favor of a weak, statewide law—by California voters indicates that the state's populace supports relatively stringent anti-tobacco measures.

At the local level, a number of barriers to more effective implementation and enforcement of tobacco control laws were identified by the respondents. For example, in both Los Angeles and Contra Costa counties many of the local ordinances failed to specify enforcement mechanisms. As a result, enforcement fell, by default, on the city attorney's office in those communities, which may or may not have viewed tobacco control as a priority issue. A longtime anti-tobacco advocate in the state indicated that it was often the case that after an ordinance was enacted "there was no plan in place for what to do next."

A second barrier noted by a number of individuals concerned the notion that AB-13 has effectively supplanted the desire of local communities to pass ordinances that contain provisions that are more stringent than those found in this act, because the city councils believe that the state law has taken care of the problem and/or they are reluctant to go beyond it. One interviewee noted that this phenomenon posed perhaps the greatest potential barrier to providing the state's residents with additional protection from tobacco smoke.

He summed up his view by stating that "AB-13 has taken the wind out of people's sails for additional ordinances."[1] This view of the effects of AB-13 is supported by data on the number of local ordinances passed in recent years. In 1993, a total of 68 local tobacco control ordinances relating to clean indoor air and/or youth access were passed throughout California; by 1995, the year that AB-13 first took effect, that number had dwindled to 12 (Hobart, personal communication).

An official from a statewide health organization indicated that a significant barrier to AB-13's implementation was that the law contains a number of provisions that are vague and difficult to interpret. (This individual cited as an example the way in which the law treats establishments that are composed of both a bar and a restaurant.) According to this observer, the law's ambiguity has caused a number of city attorneys to tell code enforcement officers not to issue citations because, if challenged, the citations would never hold up in a court of law.

New York State

New York State has all the pieces in place to mount a sustained effort to implement and enforce tobacco control laws. From a legislative perspective, New York State has one of the strongest statewide clean indoor air acts in the United States. Although the Pataki administration appears to be more sympathetic to the tobacco industry's continuing efforts to enact preemption, the tobacco industry has not been able to impose its legislative agenda. There are also a number of stringent local anti-tobacco ordinances that in some instances exceed the state's requirements. These ordinances have considerable local political support. And there are several active statewide and local anti-tobacco coalitions. Yet this array of factors has not resulted in a cohesive implementation and enforcement effort.

State-Level Activity. Two general themes characterize the New York State enforcement program. One theme is that enforcement is

---

[1]This, however, may be a natural but temporary phenomenon. As one interviewee in New York noted, the New York statewide law initially inhibited the development of local ordinances. As time wore on, discontent over exceptions contained in the state law eventually led locales to adopt stronger regulations.

largely delegated to local health departments. When the 1989 Clean Indoor Air Act (CIAA) was being debated, there was a trade-off for its enactment. At the expense of enforcement, the legislature mandated that local health departments would enforce the CIAA, not the state department of health. This was extended to youth access. At the state level, the New York State Department of Health therefore focuses on implementing Project ASSIST and providing educational materials to anti-tobacco coalitions.

The second theme is the fragmented nature of implementation responsibilities. No one agency has overall authority or responsibility for tobacco control activities. Even within statutes, enforcement authority is extremely fragmented. License removal or suspension can occur only at the state level. Thus, if a local health department wants to remove a vendor's tobacco license after repeated violations, it must obtain cooperation from the New York State Department of Tax and Finance.

Local Activity. We visited four local health departments, each of which is responsible for enforcing both the statewide clean indoor air laws as well as strong local ordinances. Regarding enforcement of the state law, a major concern expressed by local health departments is that this amounts to an unfunded mandate: "Tell [us] what you want us to stop doing if you want [us] to enforce this." In short, whatever clean indoor air enforcement occurs results from enforcing the local ordinance, not from enforcing the state law.[2] In two of the four local sites, the county health department includes a smoking check on routine restaurant compliance checks, but otherwise the local health departments respond only to clean indoor air complaints.

All four of our local sites have conducted sting operations to reduce tobacco sales to minors. Each of the local sites has indicated an intention to be an aggressive enforcement agency in reducing youth access to tobacco products. In New York City, the Department of Consumer Affairs conducted 196 stings pursuant to a city ordinance

---

[2]It is possible that this finding is an artifact of our sampling strategy in which each sampled county has enacted an ordinance. In counties without such ordinances, the county health department would respond to complaints alleging violations of state laws.

in April 1996. During the stings, 47 percent of vendors illegally sold cigarettes to minors, down from 63 percent in a previous sting. However, 18 vendors violated the ordinance for the third time and face license suspension proceedings.

Relationship Between State and Local Laws. Unlike preemption states, the relationship between state and local tobacco control laws and agencies is difficult to characterize. In a sense, they occupy parallel universes with less interaction than we had anticipated. Absent preemption, local municipalities can, and do, enact tobacco control measures more stringent than the state law. Subsequent to the 1989 statewide Clean Indoor Air Act, local municipalities, including New York City and Suffolk and Westchester Counties, enacted stronger local anti-tobacco ordinances. And because enforcement is largely delegated to local health departments, the state agencies function more as educational and funding conduits than as close partners in implementing tobacco control laws.

As already noted, the state's tobacco control regulatory mechanism is highly fragmented, strengthening any local municipality that wants to undertake aggressive enforcement activities. There appears to be only limited coordination between state and local officials on enforcement activities or strategies. According to local officials, the fragmentation is particularly problematic in seeking to suspend or remove a vendor's license because state approval is necessary.

Stakeholders' Roles. Mirroring the fragmented enforcement efforts at the state and local levels, there are two statewide anti-tobacco coalitions and a number of independent local coalitions. They appear to have one thing in common: a focus on legislation and a limited enforcement agenda. According to our interviews, local coalitions in our sample have had only limited activity in enforcement and implementation. As one respondent trenchantly noted, "It is hard to sustain interest in a local coalition after a few meetings or successes. This is an endemic problem with no easy fix." Nor have the coalitions pressured the state department of health to allocate more money to tobacco control enforcement. But at least one local coalition in our sample has been active in merchant education and in recruiting volunteers for compliance checks.

By all accounts, the tobacco industry's presence remains primarily at the legislative level, with very little involvement in enforcement and implementation. The exception to this is the tobacco industry's aggressive "We Card" program. To the limited extent that respondents noted tobacco industry involvement in enforcement and implementation, the primary opposition strategy appears to be to work through individual restaurateurs and the New York State Restaurant and Tavern Association.

In general, retail merchants have not actively opposed implementation and enforcement in New York State. As with the tobacco industry, retail merchants focus on legislative lobbying, especially to obtain preemption. Several officials in local municipalities stated that retail merchants' groups have sent mailings to local merchants asking them to post signs and to become familiar with the laws but are not aware of any training or education conducted by merchants' groups.

Barriers to Enforcement. Our interviews revealed several barriers to effective implementation and enforcement in New York. With respect to both clean indoor air and youth access, the first barrier is that enforcement is not a high priority with local health departments. School violence, child abuse, and other such issues are more important responsibilities. Local governments are crisis oriented, while smoking is an ongoing problem. The second barrier is the lack of resources at the local level to sustain an enforcement effort. Many respondents noted that tobacco control enforcement amounts to an unfunded mandate for local health departments.

We also identified two barriers that apply specifically to youth access. One is the lack of coordination between licensure and enforcement. Two different state agencies are responsible for overseeing vendor licensing and for taking action to suspend or remove a license. Coordinating local enforcement activity with two different agencies makes license suspension needlessly complex. Additionally, the tobacco industry's promotional schemes encourage sales to minors, including displays, slotting fees, ads, and reimbursement for lost sales. Finally, the structure of fines in the legislation is a problem. It takes three violations before a license is lost, but with high turnover in ownership (especially at bodegas), this means starting over each time. Also owners beat the system by changing their establishments' names.

Two additional barriers pertain to implementing and enforcing clean indoor air laws. First, restaurant owners are reluctant to enforce the laws, as are waiters who fear they may lose tips. Second, the public is often unaware of the law's provisions, particularly those governing smoking in restaurants, or of the procedures for filing a complaint.

Illinois

As the price for obtaining a statewide clean indoor air act in 1989, Illinois anti-tobacco advocates had to accept a provision preempting local municipalities from enacting more stringent tobacco control ordinances. Yet corresponding enforcement authority was not granted to the appropriate state agency, and despite an active statewide coalition, enforcement in Illinois has languished.

State-Level Activity. There are two general themes that characterize the Illinois state-level enforcement program. One theme is the absence of statutory enforcement authority. Although the 1989 Illinois Clean Indoor Air Act (CIAA) preempts stronger local anti-tobacco initiatives, parallel enforcement authority has not been granted to state agencies. In fact, neither the CIAA nor its youth access law provides for state-level enforcement responsibility, essentially delegating enforcement to local agencies. As a result, the Illinois Department of Public Health (IDPH), with nominal jurisdiction over clean indoor air regulations, and the Illinois Liquor Control Commission (ILCC), which is responsible for compliance with the state's youth access restrictions, undertake no enforcement activities.

The second theme is the fragmented nature of implementation responsibilities. No one agency has overall authority or responsibility for tobacco control activities. Under ILCC's five-year Synar plan, for instance, separate departments will be designated as lead agencies for Synar enforcement. IDPH will be the lead agency on Synar education, and the Department of Alcohol and Substance Abuse will also have limited Synar responsibility for schools. No agency appears to have authority to suspend tobacco licenses. As an Illinois Coalition Against Tobacco (ICAT) member observed, "Local health departments are key to enforcement in Illinois. Local health departments in Illinois are autonomous, with loyalty to local politicians."

Most respondents in Illinois believe that the CIAA is self-enforcing, driven by cultural changes. For youth access, respondents believe that enforcement is necessary and can be effective. In any event, there is little overt enforcement activity of either law outside of Chicago and Woodridge, and almost none at the state level. At this point, tobacco control enforcement in Illinois amounts to an unfunded mandate. At the state level, noted one observer, "Smoking remains a low visibility issue, where state intervention is not taken seriously."

Local Activity. As noted previously, the preemption provision in the Illinois' CIAA limits the incentives for local municipalities to enact separate clean indoor air regulations. Although local municipalities can enforce either the state's CIAA or the state's youth access law, our interviews with knowledgeable respondents indicated that only two local jurisdictions were actively involved in enforcement and implementation activities: Chicago and Woodridge. Most county health departments have not initiated efforts to enforce the state anti-tobacco law systematically. For example, few county health departments have included smoking on the checklist for restaurant inspections.

Stakeholder Roles. Our interviews consistently revealed that ICAT's primary organizing principle is to enact legislation, with enforcement and implementation as secondary activities. A typical comment from coalition respondents was

> Up until now, the coalition has not focused on implementation or enforcement. Currently, the coalition remains focused on developing statewide legislation and local ordinances. It is easier for a coalition to rally around legislation than around implementation. Enforcement is a police mentality and could be counterproductive if taken too far.

Another respondent added that "the long-term nature of implementation can be frustrating . . ., advancing only in incremental steps."

More specifically, our interviews indicate that only two particular coalition members are focusing on enforcement at this time. For example, they are currently developing a training manual and workshop for local communities interested in tobacco control enforcement. Implementation is a process of building alliances, but right now, the coalition is more focused on legislation than on building alliances and community support for implementation.

According to our interviews, the tobacco industry does not play an overt role in enforcement or implementation. Instead, the tobacco industry relies on governmental inertia resulting from the laws' nature as unfunded mandates. There is not much direct tobacco industry opposition to actual enforcement because it can defeat stronger legislation. If the strength of enforcement provisions is limited, the tobacco industry does not need to worry about implementation.

The Illinois Retail Merchants' Association (IRMA) has taken the lead in opposing additional restrictions on youth access, arguing that the legislation is already burdensome to merchants. Its primary argument is that before adding any significant changes in sanctions against sellers, IRMA wants similar sanctions on users—a balance of sanctions against the seller and the buyer. As one respondent noted, "An underage user should face similar stings, penalties, and public scorn as the retailer if fined or sanctioned." IRMA's position is that underage smoking should be treated just the same as underage alcohol consumption.

Barriers to Implementation and Enforcement. With only minor exceptions, barriers to enforcement and implementation detected in our Illinois interviews do not vary between state and local agencies. Not surprisingly, the most consistent barriers mentioned for both the CIAA and youth access are bureaucratic inertia and the lack of resources required to enforce either law. In reality, smoking is a low priority for most agencies.

Florida

Relationship Between State and Local Laws. As in Illinois, the historical relationship between Florida's statewide anti-tobacco legislation and local ordinances can be characterized by one word: preemption. There is little local activity, and our interviews revealed virtually no attempts to enact local ordinances, except in West Palm Beach. Indeed, state law prohibits local ordinances that are stronger than state law, effectively undermining any sustained local efforts to enact anti-tobacco ordinances. Although local municipalities could expand enforcement activities based on state law, it seems clear that preemption undercuts virtually all local tobacco control activity. Respondents indicated that local officials look to the state for tobacco enforcement, especially since only the state can bring an administrative action for license removal.

State-Level Activity. The absence of any local enforcement activity places the burden of enforcement on the responsible state agencies. With regard to youth access, there is a sustained enforcement effort. For the clean indoor air act, the state largely relies on voluntary compliance. As in most states in our sample, enforcement responsibility is fragmented across various agencies, with little communication or coordination regarding strategies, goals, or methods.

By all accounts, the Florida Division of Alcohol, Beverages, and Tobacco (ABT), the designated youth access enforcement agency, has moved aggressively to reduce cigarette sales to minors. Tobacco enforcement is a priority for ABT and is an important part of its strategic goals. According to one state official, "ABT has invested considerable manpower, money, and time in the program." The division's strategic plan calls for each of the three district offices to sting 80 percent of tobacco vendors. Local police agencies can also enforce over-the-counter tobacco sales to minors, although few have done so outside of joint demonstrations with ABT.

The Florida Department of Health and Rehabilitation Services (HRS), the state agency responsible for enforcing the state's clean indoor air act, relies exclusively on public complaints to enforce Florida's CIAA. Until recently, HRS had only one position for the entire state to enforce the act, but now a second position has been added. Although the state's CIAA enforcement mechanism appears to rely almost entirely on voluntary compliance, it is important to point out that coalition respondents believe that HRS has been responsive within the limits of its resources. Thus, many respondents believe that the law has had some impact despite low enforcement levels.

Local Activity. As noted above, we found no independent local implementation or enforcement activity. Local agencies were reluctant to enforce state law, and preemption eliminated any local ordinances to enforce.

Stakeholder Roles. Florida has an active statewide anti-tobacco coalition, Tobacco-Free Florida (TFF), along with several local coalitions organized under the aegis of TFF. Our interviews suggest that TFF's primary focus is legislative, with a secondary emphasis on education, while deferring to public agencies to enforce the laws. TFF has no current strategies for enforcement, such as local surveys of restaurants or pressure on local businesses.

A major TFF activity is to organize local coalitions to contact local legislators. As an organizing strategy, the coalition is emphasizing youth access restrictions. TFF hopes to empower youth to take on the tobacco industry. An additional plan is to increase teacher awareness of tobacco control issues through teacher training on tobacco.

The tobacco industry's primary strategy appears to be to hang onto preemption. There is no indication that the industry is active at the local level or is attempting to undermine implementation efforts. Other than organized opposition to Florida's litigation against tobacco companies to recover Medicaid costs, there has been no organized tobacco industry response to implementation. In schools, the industry is promoting "We Don't Want Kids to Smoke"—that smoking is an adult habit or choice.

For the most part, retail merchants do not appear to be involved in enforcement and implementation activities. TFF and the local coalitions report little communication with retail merchants' associations, and the associations do not appear to provide educational materials on tobacco control for their members. Initially, ABT received complaints from retail merchants that the sting operations amounted to entrapment, but now ABT reports receiving good cooperation from merchants on over-the-counter sales. As one ABT field officer noted, "No one wants to be on record as okay to sell to minors."

Barriers to Enforcement. Most respondents noted that the major barriers to enforcing both types of laws are the lack of resources, preemption, and the lack of public awareness and education. Aside from the educational barrier, which coalitions can address, no one indicated that the other barriers would change any time soon.

More than in any other state in our sample, the issue of penalizing youths for possessing cigarettes is a major topic of discussion in Florida. As one enforcement officer observed,

> No matter how hard the investigation, kids will continue to buy cigarettes and alcohol—kids will obtain them. Because there are no statutory provisions against possession, there is no way to get to the juvenile. We can make all the sales arrests and it won't affect sales to minors. Absent sanctions for possession, there are no sanctions to stop the behavior.

The respondent went on to argue that tobacco control requires the same law enforcement strategies that are used to reduce car theft, juvenile delinquency, and alcohol consumption.

Chapter Three

RESULTS

HOW ARE TOBACCO CONTROL LAWS IMPLEMENTED AND ENFORCED?

Implementation Versus Enforcement

During our interviews, respondents consistently distinguished between implementation and enforcement. Enforcement relates to the narrow range of potential sanctions contained in state legislation or local ordinances, such as license removal, fines, or conducting sting operations, resulting from specific law enforcement activity. Enforcement thus refers to actions required by law that are monitored by state and local officials. Alternatively, respondents viewed implementation as a much broader term, encompassing educational activities, dissemination of materials by stakeholders, and developing processes to ensure compliance with state and local tobacco control laws.

To a certain extent, this is a somewhat artificial distinction. Many respondents view enforcement as one part of a broader implementation strategy. As one respondent stated, "Vendor education has worked to a degree, but accountability, through enforcement, is required." Nonetheless, the distinction offers a useful construct for this report.

Clean Indoor Air Laws

State Enforcement Activity. The overwhelming consensus among respondents was that state clean indoor air laws are self-enforcing and that they will not be systematically enforced by state or local authorities.[1] By self-enforcing, we mean that people voluntarily comply with the law in the absence of a systematic enforcement effort. Regardless of either the specified enforcement provisions or the existence of preemption, state clean indoor air laws are not rigorously enforced at the state level in our sample states. In fact, states allocate few resources for enforcing clean indoor air laws.

In our sample, enforcement of any state clean indoor air law is generally delegated to local health departments, except in California. The ironic result is that we observed little difference in state-level enforcement activity between states with strong statewide anti-tobacco laws, states that preempt stronger local ordinances, and states with no statewide anti-tobacco legislation.

Preemption States. In both of the preemption states, Florida and Illinois, there is only minimal enforcement activity by state agencies. In Florida, for example, there are only two people in the state enforcement office for the entire state. Even though anti-tobacco coalition respondents conceded that the office was attempting to enforce the law, they also indicated that current staffing limitations prevented all but nominal responses to complaints. During 1994, the state agency in Florida received 309 complaints, closed 210 of them through voluntary compliance, made 32 on-site inspections, and initiated 4 administrative proceedings.

In Illinois, the department of public health (IDPH) lacks statutory enforcement authority. Like Florida, IDPH relies on voluntary compliance. IDPH's role is to provide technical assistance to local health departments, including educational materials, rather than to conduct enforcement activity. For instance, the department develops information packets, such as fact sheets, signs, and press releases, that are targeted to specific organizations. In essence, IDPH serves an implementation rather than an enforcement function. Any

---

[1]It is important to note, however, that most state and local enforcement mechanisms are "complaint-driven." That is, while the designated enforcement agency does not typically attempt to enforce the law in a deliberate or proactive manner, it does respond to complaints made against establishments by individuals. Although the complaint process is an important ingredient to a successful enforcement program, widespread voluntary compliance with clean indoor air laws is critical to keeping the complaints generated down to a manageable number.

enforcement activity is therefore delegated to local health departments.

Strong State Laws. Even in the sample states with strong statewide anti-tobacco laws, enforcement by state agencies is minimal. By statute in New York, all enforcement of the state's clean indoor air law is delegated to county health departments, except in certain rural areas where the state department of health retains enforcement jurisdiction. Two separate local health department respondents characterized the state's enforcement strategy as "benign neglect," in part because tobacco control goals have not previously been an aspect of the local health departments' contract with the state.

In Minnesota, the Department of Health's Division of Environmental Health devotes one full-time equivalent (FTE) employee to coordinating and administering the various provisions of the state law and delegates enforcement responsibility, especially for restaurants, to over 40 local health agencies. The state receives approximately 100 complaints per year, but only two administrative penalty orders have been issued. By all accounts, the law is largely self-enforcing.

Although California now has a strong state law, its preemption provision is ambiguous and has yet to be clarified by the courts or the legislature. Unlike Florida and Illinois, the California provision establishes a minimum level of tobacco control but allows local governments to impose additional restrictions on areas left unregulated by state law. Nevertheless, the act requires that the law be enforced by a local law enforcement agency, such as the police department or local health department, as determined by local officials. At this point, the state has played a limited role in implementing the act, providing little or no training to local agencies and little support generally.

Local Enforcement Activity. Our results indicate considerable activity at the local level to implement and enforce CIAA provisions. Most of that activity, however, revolves around enforcing local ordinances rather than state laws.

Local Enforcement of State Laws. The willingness and ability of local agencies to enforce state clean indoor air laws vary in our sample but are generally quite limited. A major concern expressed by local health departments in New York, Minnesota, California, and Illinois is that this amounts to an unfunded mandate: "Tell us what you want us to stop doing if you want to enforce this." Equally important, as suggested above, states provide little nonfinancial support for local enforcement. Despite the Illinois Department of Public Health's stated goal of providing educational materials for local health departments, respondents at the Chicago Department of Health indicated that they have no relations with IDPH on tobacco control.

Thus, few local agencies actively enforce state clean indoor air laws beyond responding to complaints. Routine compliance checks are rare, except for including smoking on a checklist for code violations in restaurant inspections in New York City, various counties in New York State, and in Chicago. Indeed, our California results suggest that 25 cities within Los Angeles County are intentionally ignoring the statewide law, preferring to rely on local ordinances. Some tobacco control advocates are encouraging local governments to retain existing clean indoor air ordinances rather than revising them to be consistent with the new statewide law (Ellis, Hobart, and Reed, 1995).

Local Enforcement of Local Laws. In several instances, including the city of Chicago and Suffolk and Chatauqua Counties in New York, local health departments have opted to enforce their own local ordinances instead of the state law. But like their state counterparts, local agencies consistently rely on voluntary compliance. With the exception of compliance checks in New York (now discontinued), clean indoor air ordinance enforcement efforts in our sample are entirely complaint driven. As with the state clean indoor air laws, these local ordinances are self-enforcing.

In the California localities we sampled, a complaint-driven response system has been sufficient to generate compliance. Few complaints have been received in Los Angeles or Contra Costa Counties, and in virtually every instance a letter from the enforcement agency "was enough to get the problem resolved." This is also the experience of New York State.

Data collection on the number and disposition of complaints is variable, but mostly lacking at the local level. In Chicago, the department of health has no reliable data on the number of complaints or how they are resolved. Most of the local officials admitted that the data on complaints and sanctions are not consistently maintained. However, the New York City Department of Health is establishing an on-line system of monitoring complaints.

Laws Restricting Youth Access to Tobacco

In contrast to the implementation and enforcement of clean indoor air laws, states and localities in our sample have been much more aggressive in enforcing laws restricting youth access to tobacco. Our interviews revealed that the primary difference is a consistent belief that youth access laws will not be self-enforcing, thus requiring a greater enforcement effort than is needed for clean indoor air regulations. Since everyone agrees that youths should not smoke, the applicable regulatory question is what mechanisms work best to limit youth access to tobacco products.

As indicated above, states have long restricted smoking to individuals above a certain age, usually 18. The state laws designed specifically to enforce youth access restrictions to tobacco products in our sample were all enacted in response to the federal Synar Amendment. We also refer to the state laws enacted in response to the Synar Amendment as Synar laws.

State Enforcement Activity. Although each of our sample states has begun a Synar program, there is wide variation in their progress and in how extensive the enforcement activity has been. For instance, New York is still at the planning stage, California only recently promulgated Synar regulations, while Florida has been active for nearly two years. We do not detect any patterns across our sample states in how they have responded to the Synar requirements, except that all states in our sample but Illinois rely or plan to rely on police stings using underage purchasers to detect noncompliance.[2]

Our states also vary with respect to the assigned Synar enforcement responsibility, but our results suggest that the nature of the assignment does not predict enforcement activity. For example, Synar was

---

[2]Our survey of state Synar enforcement is only one aspect of our overall project. We refer readers to ongoing work conducted by Shoshanna Sofaer at George Washington University, Washington, D.C., pursuant to a Robert Wood Johnson Foundation grant to study all states' responses to the federal Synar Amendment.

delegated to the equivalent agencies in Florida and Illinois, but Florida has been much more committed to Synar compliance activities than has Illinois. Thus, our results provide little guidance on the most effective locus of Synar responsibility.

In our sample, the assignment of responsibility is not necessarily a function of which agency stands to lose block grant funds if the state fails to comply with federal Synar requirements. More important, our results indicate that Synar responsibility is often delegated to agencies with little or no experience in working with tobacco control issues. This delegation occurs in agencies in Illinois, Minnesota, Texas, and New York, which require the agency to contract with other agencies that have more relevant experience. As we discuss below, this contributes to the overall fragmentation of responsibility that characterizes state-level tobacco control activity.

The most active Synar state in our sample is Florida. By all accounts, the Division of Alcohol, Beverages, and Tobacco (ABT), the designated Synar enforcement agency, has aggressively moved to reduce cigarette sales to minors. Indeed, tobacco enforcement is a priority strategic goal for ABT. The agency has invested considerable staff, money, and time in implementation, including an education program for vendors and training for employees. Each ABT office has also aggressively moved to enforce the law through stings. ABT's strategic plan calls for each of the district offices to sting 80 percent of tobacco vendors. Locations are selected based on previous information (i.e., complaints). At three recent strikes, ABT recorded a 20 percent noncompliance rate, but one of the regional offices we visited showed a 35 percent noncompliance rate, with considerable day-to-day fluctuation. So far, no licenses have been revoked, though fines have been collected.

The least active state in our sample with respect to youth access activities is Illinois, through the Illinois Liquor Control Commission (ILCC), which has not gone beyond surveying vendors. Although ILCC plans certain implementation activities, such as vendor education through a video, the agency lacks the authority to enforce the youth access law. Any enforcement will result from local police department efforts.

Both Texas and Arizona, states with no statewide clean indoor air laws, have begun to implement youth access provisions. Arizona initiated a set of pilot projects in three local areas to conduct unannounced inspections, educate vendors, and survey teenagers. In Texas, the state has contracted with Drug Abuse Resistance Education (DARE) to train over 650 DARE officers on the health effects of tobacco use, state law governing the sale of tobacco to minors, and methods for conducting compliance checks. The Texas Department of Health conducted a baseline survey showing a 56 percent noncompliance rate for over-the-counter sales, rising to 93 percent for vending machine violations. Neither state has initiated any formal enforcement activities.

It is somewhat surprising that the states in our sample with strong statewide CIAA provisions, Minnesota and New York, have been slow to develop a state-level Synar enforcement program. Minnesota's Synar-related efforts have been limited to requesting information from cities and counties that have conducted sting operations on the results of those operations, contracting with the University of Minnesota's School of Public Health to conduct a survey of municipalities on their ordinance enforcement activities, and contracting with the Association for Nonsmokers—Minnesota (ANSR) to provide random unannounced compliance checks of vendors in the Twin Cities area. In New York, Synar activity is currently at the planning stages. The relevant agency is conducting a survey and preparing a compliance protocol for subsequent enforcement activities.

Local Enforcement Activity. In contrast to local activity regarding clean indoor air enforcement, we found considerably greater local involvement in youth access law enforcement. Although our results suggest that smaller municipalities are more likely to initiate compliance stings, both New York and Chicago have committed resources to Synar compliance. We found no Synar-related activity at local sites visited in California, Texas, and Florida.

The most consistent local enforcement in our sample is in Woodridge, Illinois, a widely studied model. What sets Woodridge apart is not so much the results, but the consistent commitment of local officials to stop tobacco sales to minors. Despite four yearly compliance checks, noncompliance rates varied between 7 and 25 percent in 1994 (which were lower than Woodridge's comparable results for alcohol sales to minors). Nevertheless, Woodridge has taken a policy position that reducing tobacco use by minors is a priority. If smoking is unchecked at an early age, Woodridge believes that it will lead to long-term substance abuse problems. Woodridge also takes the position that a license to do business in Woodridge is a privilege, not a right. Merchants must follow the rules, similar to motor vehicle laws, but a constant enforcement presence is needed to ensure compliance.

We found a similar approach in Suffolk and Chatauqua Counties, New York. One official reinforced the importance of constant enforcement pressure in commenting on the fact that Suffolk County had checked only 250 out of 2,000 tobacco vendors in three years:

> There are short bursts of compliance activity and then regression. DOH [the department of health] needs to conduct random compliance checks 52 weeks per year. Ongoing compliance checks are necessary. It will not be self-enforcing, and there have been no changes in merchants' attitudes.

An important experiment that extends the Woodridge approach is a regional strategy adopted by suburbs located north of the Twin Cities in Minnesota. Unlike the Woodridge and Chatauqua strategies, the North Suburban Compliance Project strategy confronts the issue of border crossing by teenagers to neighboring communities that do not vigorously enforce state laws on selling cigarettes to minors. The project conducts a series of regular compliance checks of all tobacco vendors in the participating communities and reports on the results of the compliance checks to the appropriate city councils. After an educational program for vendors was mounted, the baseline rate of illegal purchases in the five original project communities was 25.4 percent. The corresponding figure for the project's second year fell to 19.5 percent (Weigum, 1995).

In contrast to the ability of smaller communities to monitor tobacco sales to minors, the large cities in our sample undertook correspondingly smaller enforcement efforts. For instance, New York City's Department of Consumer Affairs allocates eight tobacco inspectors to two yearly compliance inspections of at least 180 tobacco vendors. Data from the most recent sting operations show a noncompliance rate of 47 percent. So far, eight licenses have been suspended, with 10 other cases pending.

In Chicago, the Chicago Department of Revenue is conducting a pilot study of 120 out of 6,000 stores in the city to determine how efficient ticketing merchants is in reducing cigarette sales to minors, and how frequently stings will result in ticketing. Some stores were inspected every two months, others every four months, others every six months, and there was a control group. Each level (including the control group) received the same educational materials. The sales rates to minors was 25 percent for the two-month group, 40 percent for the four-month group, 60 percent for the six-month group, and 95 percent for the control stores. The initial baseline visit revealed an 80 percent illegal sales rate overall. The pilot program is unlikely to be extended because preliminary results suggest that it is hard to generate sufficient program benefits to justify the enforcement costs in a city with a high crime rate.

Fragmented Enforcement Authority

One of the structural difficulties that may help explain the results of our case studies is that enforcement authority is highly fragmented across several agencies in our sample states, making it difficult to communicate and coordinate goals, strategies, or enforcement methods. This fragmentation is especially apparent in New York and Illinois.

In New York, for example, no one agency has overall authority or responsibility for tobacco control activities. Even within statutes, enforcement authority is extremely fragmented. For example, under Synar, the Office of Alcohol and Substance Abuse Service (OASAS) has responsibility for evaluating Synar compliance, the New York State Department of Health (NYSDOH) has responsibility for Synar enforcement, monitoring, and imposing civil fines; while the New York State Department of Tax and Finance has control over licenses. Though dependent on these other state agencies, OASAS loses federal funds if the state does not comply with Synar. License removal or suspension can occur only at the state level. Enforcing Synar requires a high degree of cooperation across state agencies. If a local health department wants to remove a vendor's tobacco license after repeated violations, it must obtain cooperation from the tax and finance department.

Penalizing Teens for Smoking

An issue that emerged in our interviews is whether underage purchasers or users should be penalized for possessing and using tobacco products. While the issue was most directly presented in our Illinois, Florida, and Minnesota interviews, the issue was present to some degree in all of the sample states, suggesting that it might gain policy salience in the future. (Minnesota passed a law in 1992 that prohibits the purchase or possession of cigarettes by minors, but by all accounts, it goes largely unenforced.) Representatives of merchants' associations were most likely to raise it as a fairness issue, but some anti-tobacco coalition members also suggested the need to fine the user to deter underage tobacco consumption.

For example, the Illinois Retail Merchants Association (IRMA) argues that there should be a balance of sanctions against the seller and the buyer. As one respondent remarked,

> An underage user should face similar stings, penalties, and public scorn as the retailer if fined or sanctioned. At what point does the responsibility of government and purveyors of legal products stop and the responsibility of parents begin?

IRMA's position is that underage smoking should be treated just the same as underage alcohol consumption.

Even though most anti-tobacco coalition respondents and state officials rejected this position, a small minority of nonindustry respondents support penalizing teens. Individual members of Tobacco-Free Florida favoring this approach want to impose a small fine or community service requirement. State officials mentioned the advisability, from an enforcement perspective, of penalizing both a merchant and the minor for illegal tobacco purchases. So far, the coalition has steadfastly opposed this approach. To most respondents, such a policy essentially penalizes the victim and is therefore anathema.

Nevertheless, some jurisdictions are beginning to address the issue. Each year, for instance, Woodridge annually issues about 10 to 15 tickets to children—a $25 fine. Woodridge does not treat children's smoking or attempting to purchase cigarettes as a major offense, in part because kids can quickly dispose of the cigarette. The mayor has received no complaints about this aspect of the program. The basic message to kids is: "Don't try to buy in Woodridge, go elsewhere." A similar approach to smoking on school grounds is under way in Suffolk County, New York. Where fines ($50) have been instituted, smoking on school grounds has declined.

RELATIONSHIP BETWEEN STATEWIDE LEGISLATION AND LOCAL ORDINANCES

A critical strategy decision faced by tobacco control advocates is whether to focus their efforts to enact clean indoor air laws, in particular, at the state or local level. This decision presents a clear tradeoff. On the one hand, statewide legislation offers the prospect of enacting a law that provides a uniform level of protection to all of the state's residents. Ideally, from the anti-tobacco advocates' point of view, the law would be quite stringent and would also provide local communities with the option of increasing the level of stringency by passing local ordinances (i.e., the law would not contain any preemption provisions). Such a strategy provides an efficient and effective route to both controlling smoking in a wide range of public places, including private work sites, and reducing minors' access to cigarettes.

The downside of this strategy is that, as we saw repeatedly in our seven case studies, the tobacco industry possesses substantial political power at the state level and has been enormously successful in either turning back bills that they consider to run contrary to their interests (e.g., those introduced by tobacco control advocates in Texas) or by insisting that any state bill include a preemption clause, such as those found in the Illinois and Florida clean indoor air bills.

On the other hand, a local strategy, though clearly less efficient, is less susceptible to the influences of the tobacco industry. For the most part, city council members abhor attempts by people whom they view as outsiders to influence their deliberations, particularly in light of the fact that their campaigns do not require significant sums of money. In addition to blunting the effects of the tobacco industry, a local strategy also helps ensure that the ordinances passed will be more responsive to the needs of particular communities than is necessarily the case with a statewide bill.

Statewide Legislation and Local Ordinances: A Two-Way Street

Suffice it to say that the debate among anti-tobacco advocates on the preferred legislative strategy is far from settled. In our case studies, however, it became evident that a complex interplay exists between statewide and local laws, with each influencing the prospects and shape of the other. For example, as we have seen in New York State, several "downstate" counties (including Westchester and Suffolk) passed clean indoor air laws that went above and beyond the state law that was enacted five years earlier. In California, we observed that the large number of local ordinances passed throughout the state over a 10-year period created a political environment that was receptive to a statewide bill (i.e., AB-13) that largely curtailed smoking in the workplace. Interestingly, in California, local ordinance development got a boost from Proposition 99, a statewide ballot initiative that increased the cigarette excise tax by 25 cents per pack and used a portion of the proceeds to fund tobacco education and research programs, which indirectly led to the formation of local coalitions and the enactment of ordinances.

Through our site visits, we found that relatively stringent statewide legislation often had an inhibitory effect on local ordinances, but that the reverse was not true. That is, again with the exception of some downstate New York counties, we found that local communities were not generally inclined to pass clean indoor air ordinances in states that had enacted statewide laws, even if there were no preemption clauses in the bill that would have prevented them from doing so. For instance, Minnesota, which passed the nation's first Clean Indoor Air Act in 1975, has witnessed notably little activity at the local level with respect to clean indoor air ordinances. Similarly, there was a precipitous decline in the number of newly enacted clean indoor air ordinances in California after AB-13 was enacted. In light of this evidence, and based on the reports of many respondents, we can conclude that once a stringent statewide bill is passed, local legislators essentially adopt the view that the problem has been solved and thus devote their energies to other issues.

In contrast, it appears that local ordinances do not exhibit a corresponding inhibitory effect on the prospects for statewide clean indoor air laws, as evidenced in California and, to a lesser extent, New York, where Nassau County, one of the state's most populous counties, had passed a stringent clean indoor air ordinance approximately two years before the statewide law was enacted.

Enforcement Considerations

The issue of enforcement is a central concern in evaluating the relative merits of a statewide versus a local tobacco control strategy. Based on our site visits, we believe that local enforcement is a critical ingredient to the success of virtually any tobacco control effort, regardless of whether it revolves around clean indoor air or teen access. This is not to say that local ordinances are preferred to statewide legislation, but merely that statewide laws should include a local enforcement component. For example, California's clean indoor air law, AB-13, is enforced at the local level. It must be pointed out, however, that local enforcement of state laws requires that local governments be provided with adequate resources to enforce the law. One of the problems encountered to date with AB-13's implementation has been that many communities have devoted little or no resources to enforcing AB-13, because they view it as yet another unfunded mandate. One Los Angeles–based tobacco control advocate asserted that 25 cities within Los Angeles County alone are intentionally ignoring AB-13. Because the level of enforcement varies across locations, the state still has what one observer referred to as a "patchwork quilt" of protection from secondhand smoke.

Elsewhere we found that states often made no effort whatsoever to enforce tobacco control laws. All of the study states, for instance, had passed laws years ago that prohibit the sale of cigarettes to minors. Yet prior to the advent of the federal Synar Amendment, described above, no concerted enforcement effort was undertaken to restrict sales to minors. As a result, baseline surveys of sales to minors revealed high illegal sales rates, often topping 50 percent. In Arizona, for example, a baseline survey of cigarette vendors in three cities indicated that, on average, teenagers succeeded in purchasing cigarettes on 52 percent of their attempts. Similarly, a statewide survey of vendors in Texas yielded an illegal purchase rate of 56 percent for over-the-counter sales and 93 percent for vending machine sales.

Local enforcement of tobacco control laws is likely to more effective vis-à-vis a state-level approach. Cigarette vendors are much more likely to behave responsibly in the face of local community pressure, especially if it is backed by significant sanctions such as license removal. Additionally, there was widespread agreement among the respondents that, in general, state governments were less committed to enforcing tobacco control laws than local governments.

Synar Amendment

To a great extent, the federal Synar Amendment has changed the dynamics of tobacco control at both the state and local levels. Prior to the amendment, all states had laws prohibiting cigarette sales to minors, but these laws were uniformly disregarded by law enforcement officials.

The passage of federal legislation, and the concomitant threat of losing block grant funds, has forced states to begin enforcing old laws and/or to enact new ones. Until recently, when the law's final regulations were implemented, states were at a loss to determine precisely what steps needed to be taken to comply with the law's requirements. Because of the threat to reduce block grants, the law introduced a new set of players into state tobacco control arenas, who often had agendas that differed markedly from the veterans in this area. Anti-tobacco forces worry that some of these new players may intentionally or unintentionally give ground to tobacco industry interests to expedite their plans to comply with the amendment. A long-time anti-tobacco advocate cautioned that "the legacy of Synar may be preemption across the country."

Despite this threat, the Synar Amendment has in fact served as a rallying cry for progressive tobacco control states, such as Minnesota and New York, and has forced the hand of those states that have heretofore shunned responsibility for tobacco control (e.g., Texas and Arizona). In a very real sense, it has changed the tobacco control landscape by, for example, virtually institutionalizing the use of sting operations and placing on the policy agenda the prospect of passing laws that penalize minors for possessing tobacco products. While it is perhaps premature to conduct a comprehensive evaluation of the effects of the Synar Amendment, based on our case studies there should be no doubt that states have taken its requirements seriously.

The Effects of Preemption

Given the arguments made in favor of preemption, one might expect a rigorous enforcement effort at the state level to compensate for the lack of an equivalent local enforcement effort. However, we found no differences in state-level enforcement of clean indoor air laws between preemption and nonpreemption states. With respect to the Synar Amendment, the mixed experience of the preemption states matches the mixed experience of nonpreemption states. From a state-level enforcement perspective, therefore, our results indicate that preemption makes little difference.

The major difference appears to be the effects of preemption on local enforcement activities. Local enforcement in our preemption states does not substitute for the lack of state-level activity. Respondents in both Illinois and Florida indicated that the inability to enact and enforce their own local ordinance depleted the local health department's interest in enforcing the state law. More to the point, neither state provides additional resources to stimulate local enforcement efforts.

This can be seen most graphically in comparing the Arizona and Texas results with Florida and Illinois. In both Arizona and Texas, states with weak laws but no preemption, local jurisdictions have enacted and enforced their own ordinances. In Florida no local ordinance can be enacted, while in Illinois, only Chicago has enacted and enforced its own ordinance (because of grandfathering).

Another consequence of preemption in Illinois is that preemption virtually locks the state into the 1990 law, with little expectation of legislative change at the state level, and none permitted at the local level. As a result, there is no diffusion of local ordinances across municipalities: "There may be visibility in one area, but there is no place to go." To be sure, preemption does not block local enforcement, but it certainly limits what can be enforced and the sanctions that can be imposed.

Diffusion of Tobacco Control Laws Across Communities

During the site visits to the local communities, we focused a portion of our discussions on the issue of how local ordinances governing both clean indoor air and teen access diffuse across communities. In particular, we were interested in determining the extent to which systematic attempts were made to enact tobacco control ordinances in adjacent communities. The diffusion of local ordinances is an important consideration because a successful diffusion strategy may limit opportunities for "border crossing." With respect to teen access, limiting border crossing is critical. That is, a stringent ordinance and enforcement effort in one community is all but meaningless if teenagers are able to purchase cigarettes down the road.

With respect to clean indoor air, the border crossing issue is somewhat more complicated. For instance, while a stringent restaurant ordinance enacted in one community may, in principle, drive smokers to eat elsewhere, it may also attract business from nonsmoking residents of neighboring communities who desire to dine in a smokefree environment. Thus, the net effect on restaurant sales is uncertain, but given that nonsmokers outnumber smokers, nationally, by approximately three to one, the ordinance is likely to have a positive effect on the community's restaurant business.

For the most part, we did not observe any sustained diffusion activities in the study states. Although numerous city council members and city staffers in communities that had passed ordinances reported that they often spoke about their experiences with the ordinances with their peers in other communities, both within and outside of their respective states, we noted that this was typically done on an ad hoc basis.[3] In fact, the only instance we observed to the contrary was in Minnesota, where one anti-tobacco advocacy group has developed a sophisticated ordinance diffusion strategy. The

[3]It is interesting to note instances in which even highly successful smoking control programs, such as the one found in Woodridge, Illinois, which conducts four vendor compliance checks per year and fines minors caught with cigarettes in their possession, have failed to diffuse to surrounding communities.

strategy involves everything from selecting target communities that are adjacent to communities that have recently passed ordinances to providing technical assistance to communities and organizing large-scale compliance checks.

In our sample, only two local sites have addressed the border crossing problem—Contra Costa County, California, and the suburbs of St. Paul, Minnesota. These sites developed regional approaches to restricting smoking in public places and to reducing access to cigarettes by teenagers, respectively. In Contra Costa County, as far back as 1984, the voluntary health associations and the county department of health founded the Contra Costa County Smoking Education Coalition that, among other activities, developed a model ordinance that was later passed by the county and all of the county's 18 cities. The ordinance prohibited smoking in enclosed public places, a portion of all workplaces, and 40 percent of the seating capacity of restaurants that can accommodate 50 or more patrons (Ellis, Hobart, and Reed, 1995).

In the suburbs of St. Paul, Minnesota, the North Suburban Compliance Project was formed by city council members and other officials from four communities (later expanded to seven communities) to improve compliance with the state law that prohibits the sale of cigarettes to minors. The project represents a regional approach to the problem, since all of the participating communities are in north Ramsey County. A number of interviewees stressed the importance of adopting a regional approach both out of concern over youths crossing borders to neighboring communities that do not vigorously enforce the state law and out of equity concerns for merchants.

This Minnesota project conducts a series of regular compliance checks of all tobacco vendors in the participating communities and reports on the results of the checks to the appropriate city councils. The city councils, in turn, work to develop and refine ordinances that impose sanctions on violators. The ordinances are enforced by local police departments, who also participate in the project. Relative to results obtained from compliance checks in other communities, both in Minnesota and in other states, the project appears to have been quite successful in reducing the number of outlets making illegal sales. The baseline rate of illegal purchases in the five original project communities was 25.4 percent, while the corresponding figure for the project's second year fell to 19.5 percent (Weigum, 1995).

The main advantage of adopting such a regional approach is simply that city council members feel "less vulnerable," as one respondent put it, than they would have if they independently passed an ordinance. Although the economic arguments against clean indoor air ordinances, especially those pertaining to restaurants, have not been supported in the literature (see, e.g., Sciacca, Ratliff, and Pappas, 1996), they still resonate among some city council members. A regional approach helps blunt the argument by effectively creating a level playing field among neighboring communities.

STAKEHOLDER ROLES IN ENFORCEMENT AND IMPLEMENTATION

Anti-Tobacco Coalitions

Three distinct themes characterize our interviews with members of anti-tobacco coalitions. First, coalitions are organized around legislation. Their interest in implementation and enforcement is secondary. Instead, government agencies play the central role in implementation and enforcement efforts. Second, involvement in implementation and enforcement tends to be on youth access restrictions rather than on clean indoor air issues. Third, all of the coalitions discuss the importance of community education but tend to use vague, general terms, rather than presenting a coherent educational program with defined objectives.

Coalitions' Roles in Enforcement and Implementation. Our interviews consistently indicated that coalitions' primary organizing principles remain focused on legislative strategy, primarily at the state level, with implementation and enforcement as secondary activities. An Illinois coalition respondent summed it up this way:

> Up until now, the coalition has not focused on implementation or enforcement. Currently, the coalition remains focused on developing statewide legislation and local ordinances. It is easier for a coalition to rally around legislation than around implementation. Enforcement is a police mentality and could be counterproductive if taken too far.

In addition, legislation has a defined end point—there is either a clear victory or defeat.

Another Illinois coalition respondent added that "the long-term nature of implementation can be frustrating . . ., advancing only in incremental steps." Coalitions are not self-sustaining, added a New York coalition member, but need action around a specific problem and a tangible goal to sustain interest: "It is hard to sustain interest in a local coalition after a few meetings or successes. This is an endemic problem with no easy fix."

None of the coalitions in our sample has a defined implementation and enforcement strategy, such as generating complaints to the enforcement agencies or pressuring the state to allocate additional resources to tobacco control enforcement. The Tobacco-Free Florida coalition has a mandate to develop extensive implementation strategy, and several coalitions, including those in Illinois and New York, are focusing on youth access restrictions.

Yet the Tobacco-Free Florida implementation initiative remains inchoate. Under the current Tobacco-Free Florida structure, the coalition oversees local coordinators who essentially set their own nonlegislative agenda. At the time of our interviews, the local coordinators had not focused on a few selected initiatives to pursue, such as cooperating with ABT on youth access law enforcement or on encouraging the establishment of smoke-free restaurants. In the 1994–1995 Tobacco-Free Florida plan, for instance, broad goals were developed to reduce smoking by 1999, but the methods for reaching and implementing those goals were not specified. In addition, the stated goals did not include enforcement activities.

Our interviews reveal three reasons for this general abdication. First, coalition members believe that enforcement in particular, and to a lesser extent implementation, should be left largely to state and local governmental agencies. Respondents repeatedly suggested that enforcement was strictly a governmental function; they did not delve into what role the coalition might play in assisting state or local agencies even though such entities are often coalition members. This is also true in Project ASSIST states, which receive money from the National Cancer Institute to establish and coordinate the activities of local coalitions. This explains the lack of an enforcement strategy but does not explain the lack of an implementation strategy.

Second, and perhaps the explanation for why coalitions have no implementation strategy, as the above quotations from respondents make clear, sustaining coalition interest in the mundane and tedious details of implementing and enforcing the laws is not easy. If nothing else, an implementation strategy requires a long-term commitment to execute it. More to the point, local coalitions have struggled to define a coordinated implementation or enforcement initiative. In a local Florida coalition, for example, members suggested interesting individual targets of opportunity for clean indoor air initiatives, such as the local airport and stadium, but were having difficulty sustaining member interest when the airport manager rebuffed their efforts. Although the coalition had greater success with the stadium, members were as yet unable to translate the individual success into a sustainable implementation effort.

Third, several coalition members argued that enacting stronger legislation is a better use of coalition resources than assisting state agencies in implementation and enforcement. They argue that stronger enforcement sanctions in the legislation will provide greater incentives for vendors to overcome the reluctance of their clerks to enforce the restrictions on youth access.

The Focus on Youth Access. To the extent that coalitions focus on implementation or enforcement, they do so around youth access restrictions. As a New York coalition member argued,

> The most important issue in the world of tobacco is teenage smoking—nothing else is even close. If you stop replacement smoking from teenagers, you stop, or at least limit, the problem. The number of lives saved from youth access restrictions is much greater than through CIAA.

Yet even on youth access, coalitions have not moved beyond the generality of focusing on youth access to specify an implementation agenda. For example, the only objective in the Tobacco-Free Florida 1994–1995 plan dealing with youth access states that the coalition will assist the state "in the enforcement of the Children's Access to Tobacco Law by training community groups to monitor the tobacco sales to children in each Florida county." As an organizing principle, several respondents argued, preventing youth access is unassailable, but the coalition has not yet been successful at organizing to facilitate stings. In several instances, governmental agencies complained that coalitions had promised to help secure teenage volunteers for compliance stings but had been unable to do so.

In Illinois and Florida, a four-year Robert Wood Johnson Foundation grant is designed to enhance community awareness regarding smoking. Focused on preventing youth access, the grant allows each coalition to determine its own priorities among education, prevention, enforcement, media, coalition-building, or policy development. Another goal of the grant is to have the coalition work with state agencies to enforce existing laws. In both states, our interviews were conducted at the organizing stages, preventing a full assessment of the grant. But in each case, there appeared to be limited coordination and direction from the state coalition to the local coalitions.

The primary nonlegislative agenda of Tobacco-Free Florida is education, focused on schools and youth access restrictions. TFF hopes to empower youth to take on the tobacco industry and hopes to convene a statewide conference. An additional plan is to increase teacher awareness of tobacco control issues through teacher training on tobacco. In Dade County, the coalition has received little cooperation from schools, as recounted by one respondent (and echoed by many others):

> Schools do not place a high priority on restricting smoking. In particular, SCAT [Student Coalition Against Tobacco] has not been embraced by the schools. Especially in inner city areas, schools are overwhelmed by curriculum demands.

In Minnesota, Project ASSIST funds have largely been allocated toward enacting local ordinances restricting youth access to tobacco. Coalitions first conduct compliance checks and then use the results to press for local ordinances that would require licensing tobacco vendors and eliminating self-service displays. In New York State, Project ASSIST funds have also been allocated for youth access restrictions. The major activity is to fund local coalitions' participation in compliance activities regarding youth access restrictions, including supplying manpower for sting operations.

Education. Each of the coalitions stresses education as an important aspect of its activities. Based on the above distinction between enforcement and implementation, we characterize the coalitions' educational strategies as implementation activities. What emerges from our interviews is that education is an often indistinct catch-all approach, encompassing both the dissemination of materials and media campaigns.

For example, the local coalition in Tampa, Florida, has a grant from The Robert Wood Johnson Foundation to conduct a media campaign in Pinellas and Pasco Counties. The campaign focuses on community education regarding youth access to tobacco—what the laws are and how the public should be educated. According to respondents, people are not aware of what the laws are, thus the need to emphasize community education. The coalition views education as a much less intrusive way of dealing with the problem.

Fragmentation. The fragmentation noted above for state enforcement efforts is not limited to enforcement officials. Although our study was not designed to evaluate the formation and operation of anti-tobacco coalitions, we found considerable fragmentation in current coalition operations. In New York State and Florida, the coalitions are much more extensive. They are both statewide and local, are much more diffuse than during our previous study, and have little clear structural or organizational links between them. In both states, there are two statewide coalitions, with overlapping memberships and directions. The result is a lack of clearly identified targets beyond the legislative agenda. In Florida, for example, it has been difficult to operationalize the six state-level working groups into a coherent agenda for the local coalitions. In any event, there appears to be little central control at the state level over what the local coalitions target. At the local level, according to a New York State coalition member, "The coalition [members] work as independent entities, with little coalition direction or unified coalition goals. Thus, each member focuses on different issues, with different priorities and goals."

The Tobacco Industry

Although the tobacco industry continues to play a dominant role in legislative matters, our results suggest that the industry plays a minor role in enforcement and implementation once laws are enacted. To be sure, the industry tries to limit the effectiveness of tobacco control legislation by restricting the range of potential enforcement sanctions, but we found no evidence that the tobacco industry is involved in the process of implementing or enforcing the laws. In some instances, in Arizona and Texas in particular, the industry appears to have established and provided financial support for front groups (that is, smokers' rights groups and restaurant and merchants associations that sprung up overnight after an ordinance was introduced) complaining about the burden tobacco controls place on smokers, restaurateurs, or vendors. In addition, as we found in our previous study, the tobacco industry focuses most of its efforts at the state level, where it typically lobbies to pass legislation that would preempt local ordinances.

A typical example of tobacco industry behavior was found in Arizona. At the local level, the tobacco industry operated, for the most part, in a rather low-key manner, limiting the bulk of its activities during the enactment phase of the process to providing financial support to front groups and writing periodic letters to the editors of local newspapers complaining about the burdens of the ordinances. In Flagstaff, the tobacco industry's role in the entire ordinance development and implementation process was described by one observer as "subdued." Although the industry vocalized its opposition to the Flagstaff ordinance while it was under debate, and during the subsequent referendum movement, industry representatives "disappeared entirely once the referendum passed," in the words of one antitobacco advocate.

At our Texas sites, Austin and Arlington, the tobacco industry "picked up and left town," according to one observer, after the ordinances were enacted. Many observers noted that the tobacco industry fights hard to block ordinances from being enacted (or to have a state preemption law) but then moves on to the next battle once the legal outcome is determined.

Retail Merchants

Our interviews revealed considerable variation in the involvement of retail merchants associations in tobacco control enforcement and implementation. For the most part, retail merchants associations do not appear to be involved in enforcement and implementation activities, but the Illinois Retail Merchants Association (IRMA) is actively engaged in monitoring enforcement efforts. Coalitions report almost no interaction with retail merchants. Government agencies indicated that retail merchants associations were cooperative but rarely went beyond providing general information and, sometimes, signs to members. Not all associations in our sample provided informational materials to members, and only Illinois (IRMA) provided training or education to members.

In response to the Chicago Department of Revenue experiment, Illinois merchants raised the issue of entrapment. The merchants argued that they lacked the intent to sell to a minor, stating that they took "no time to look for customer identification" and that the customers looked older than 21. Initially, the Florida ABT received complaints from retail merchants that stings amounted to entrapment but now reports receiving cooperation from merchants on over-the-counter sales. As one ABT field officer noted, "No one wants to be on record as okay to sell to minors, so there's a limit on industry pressure."

In New York State and Florida, retail merchants objected to restrictions on vending machine sales, but many retailers have removed vending machines in lieu of fines. The regulatory agency overseeing vending machines in New York State indicated that vending machines in the state have been reduced by 50 percent since laws were enacted requiring line-of-sight sales from vending machines and limiting where vending machines could be located.

Restaurant Associations. Restaurant associations and restaurateurs did not play a major role in implementation and enforcement in our sample. Nevertheless, restaurant associations are not necessarily in favor of strict enforcement. The primary argument articulated in New York State and Florida is to let the market sort it out. From the restaurateurs' perspective, they are in the hospitality business of accommodating customers, and the law improperly puts the restaurateur between the smoker and the nonsmoker. A trade association representative noted that "we don't want to be perceived as supporting one group or another. We just want to run our business and take care of customers."[4] Interestingly, one association respondent confirmed what state and local restaurant inspectors claimed, that some association members are saying the law should have eliminated smoking altogether, although he added that members did not report a high demand for nonsmoking seats before the ordinance was enacted. The Florida respondent agreed, noting that members want the issue decided one way or the other.

BARRIERS TO EFFECTIVE IMPLEMENTATION AND ENFORCEMENT

We focused a considerable portion of our discussions with the respondents on identifying barriers to the effective implementation and enforcement of tobacco control laws at the state and local levels. Several unmistakable themes emerged that cut across states, local communities, and even type of tobacco control law (i.e., teen access or clean indoor air). One such theme we found particularly surprising is that the relative salience of the smoking issue in comparison with other public policy issues appeared to be low.

Salience of the Smoking Issue

Implicitly or explicitly, respondents indicated that tobacco control often failed to ignite the passions of state legislators or city council members or even the public at large. Many expressed their disappointment in the apparent unwillingness of elected officials and others to work tirelessly on enacting, implementing, and enforcing increasingly stringent anti-tobacco measures. One respondent, however, was quick to cut to the chase, saying simply that "smoking is not handguns." The general lack of passion often made it difficult for anti-tobacco activists to keep the smoking issue on the public policy agenda. Moreover, once a measure was passed, state and local elected officials appeared to be willing to set the entire issue aside for a while, reasoning that they had just done something to alleviate

---

[4]Another respondent was more direct: "If nonsmokers do not articulate their opposition, then tough—the audience is never wrong. It is not incumbent on the owner to read the customer."

the problem and that now their attention needed to be turned to other issues.

Even among anti-tobacco activists, the level of interest appeared to wane when the issue turned from enactment to implementation and enforcement. As previously noted, many anti-tobacco activists tended to focus their efforts on passing a local ordinance or a statewide bill and not on implementation and enforcement concerns. Except in New York State, where one respondent argued that implementation required expertise from public health professions (i.e., voluntary associations), we found this to be particularly true with respect to representatives from the major voluntary health associations. These associations tended to shy away from all implementation and enforcement activities. The public rationale behind their lack of involvement in these activities was that such activities should be relegated to governmental entities such as local police departments, public health agencies, and so on. Privately, however, several representatives from these organizations revealed that their failure to embrace enforcement efforts was, to a large extent, due to their reluctance to engage in possibly confrontational situations with cigarette vendors and other local merchants, who were frequently relied upon for donations. Furthermore, from an organizational perspective, work on enacting a bill or ordinance often had a tangible outcome (i.e., a new law). In contrast, it is difficult to measure the outcomes associated with efforts to implement and enforce a law.

There was virtually unanimous agreement among the respondents on the point that law enforcement officials have not accorded tobacco control a high priority. In Texas, for example, we found that even many of the DARE officers failed to embrace the importance of tobacco control, and instead focused their educational programs on the hazards associated with alcohol and illicit drugs. As one senior state official put it, "the police are the biggest barrier to effective enforcement because they don't believe that [tobacco control] is an important issue."

Additionally, there is some evidence to suggest that local health departments, too, fail to make tobacco control enforcement activities a high priority. In New York State, for instance, several respondents noted that local health departments are crisis-oriented, focusing on school violence, child abuse, spouse abuse, and so on. But smoking is an ongoing problem and, as such, is likely to get pushed to the back burner.

Resource Constraints

A second barrier to more effective implementation and enforcement frequently cited by respondents was resource constraints. The lack of adequate resources for implementation efforts has resulted in delays in enforcing the law and confusion on the part of businesses and other affected parties. An example of the problems associated with poor implementation efforts is California's experience with AB-13. In this instance and others, many of the local-level respondents indicated that they viewed the enforcement of state tobacco control laws as just another unfunded mandate.

Regarding enforcement, inadequate resources have meant that many states and local communities have undertaken no systematic and/or proactive initiatives to enforce tobacco control laws, but rather have relied almost exclusively on complaint-driven "systems." Although the presence of strong social norms against exposing individuals to passive smoke have by and large obviated the need for states and locales to actively enforce clean indoor air laws, all evidence indicates that teen access laws are decidedly not self-enforcing and that ongoing sting operations are essential to maintaining low illegal sales rates. To ensure their long-run survival, sting operations must be self-supporting. Some communities, such as Shoreview and Roseville, Minnesota, have managed to finance the costs of compliance checks by charging annual license fees to sell tobacco products.

Ultimately, the resource constraint barrier is a political one in that state and local elected officials may be unwilling to commit resources to the fight against tobacco if they believe that it is not in their own political interests to do so. As one New York State respondent put it,

> Stings are an effective enforcement mechanism if agencies have the political will to enrage merchants. It is the advocates' responsibility to make the moral arguments that to avoid enforcement is to be soft on corporate crime or that merchants who sell tobacco to children do not deserve to retain their licenses.

Fragmented Enforcement Authority

We found diffuse authority and responsibility for enforcing tobacco control laws to be a third significant barrier. In Texas, for example, no single agency has been assigned responsibility for tobacco control. Similarly, in New York State, responsibility for licensing tobacco vendors and for enforcing and implementing the state's youth access law is split between three different agencies. In many, if not most, of the states visited, the advent of the Synar Amendment has introduced an entirely new set of stakeholders into the tobacco control process who often have different (and, in general, narrower) agendas from other stakeholders.

Ambiguous Legal Authority

Another barrier to effective implementation and enforcement often noted during our interviews was the fact that the laws themselves contained ambiguous language and/or they failed to detail precisely how the law is to be enforced. According to at least one observer, in California, a number of city attorneys told their code enforcement officers not to issue citations to firms found out of compliance with AB-13, the state's law that prohibits smoking in most work sites, because, if challenged, the citations would never hold up in court because of the law's vague language. In Flagstaff, Arizona, the failure of that city's initial restaurant ordinance to clearly specify the differences between bars and restaurants led a number of restaurant owners to claim that their establishments were really bars, which were exempt from the ordinance.

Preemption

State preemption of local tobacco control laws has also proven to be a significant enforcement barrier. In states such as Illinois and Florida, we noted that preemption has sapped the enthusiasm of local officials to implement or enforce the state laws. As one such official stated, "There is a feeling of hopelessness because we cannot do anything. Preemption gives away the house and stifles local initiative."

Potential Backlash

It is important to point out that even in the unlikely event that many or all of the aforementioned barriers were suddenly lifted, tobacco control proponents would still have to walk a fine line with respect to the level of vigor they demand from enforcement efforts. Based on our interviews, we believe that stringent enforcement efforts at the state and local levels may well prove counterproductive and provoke a tobacco industry led backlash. If the tobacco industry's fabricated image of a brown-shirted "smoking police force" were in some sense to bear resemblance to reality, then we could reasonably expect them to redouble their efforts at the state level either to enact legislation overturning or seriously weakening the statewide law or to pass a law that preempts local ordinances. As one of our respondents summed up this point of view, "If you get greedy, you'll lose."

Just as important, if the image of the smoking police force becomes rooted in the public debate, public support for tobacco control may diminish. As we detailed in our previous study (Jacobson, Wasserman, and Raube, 1993), the tobacco industry has been very effective in using arguments against governmental interference to blunt stronger legislation. Overly aggressive enforcement efforts, particularly regarding clean indoor air legislation, may well produce a public backlash. At this time, however, public support for strong measures to limit teen access to cigarettes seems secure.

Chapter Four

DISCUSSION

Taken together, the results described above strongly suggest that there is a limited effort to implement and enforce tobacco control laws in our sample states. With regard to each of our study's five primary research questions, our results suggest that implementation and enforcement is, at best, a secondary concern of state and local officials and tobacco control advocates. As we discuss below, these findings have policy implications for other public health measures. Our major findings can be summarized as follows.

First, state and local clean indoor air laws are largely self-enforcing. Neither state nor local public health or law enforcement officials devote significant resources to mounting systematic enforcement efforts. In contrast, teen access laws, particularly those related to selling cigarettes to minors, require organized and sustained enforcement efforts to ensure that merchants refrain from making illegal sales. Our case study results make it abundantly clear that an ongoing enforcement effort, complete with routine compliance checks, is a necessary but not sufficient component for reducing the rate of illegal cigarette sales to minors.

Second, a complex interplay exists between statewide and local laws, with each influencing the prospects and shape of the other. We found, for instance, that relatively stringent statewide legislation often had an inhibitory effect on local ordinances, but that the reverse was not true. The issue of enforcement is a central concern in evaluating the relative merits of a statewide versus a local tobacco control strategy.

Third, four distinct themes emerged from our interviews regarding the roles played by anti-tobacco coalitions in the implementation and enforcement process: (1) coalitions are organized around legislation—their interest in implementation and enforcement is secondary; (2) coalition involvement in implementation and enforcement tends to be on youth access restrictions rather than on clean indoor air issues; (3) all of the coalitions discuss the importance of community education but tend to do so in vague, general terms, rather than presenting a coherent educational program with defined objectives; and (4) coalitions exert little pressure on enforcement agencies to expand or accelerate enforcement efforts.

Fourth, although the tobacco industry continues to play a dominant role in legislative matters, our results suggest that the industry plays a minor role in enforcement and implementation once laws are enacted. To be sure, the industry tries to limit the effectiveness of tobacco control legislation by restricting the range of potential enforcement sanctions, but we found no evidence that the tobacco industry interferes with the process of implementing or enforcing the laws.

Fifth, an overwhelming majority of respondents made the same recommendation regarding increasing the effectiveness of various enforcement mechanisms: Keep them simple. This recommendation applied to both clean indoor air and teen access measures. Moreover, the respondents recommended that all aspects of the enforcement mechanism—including where authority is vested, the structure of the penalties, the source of funds for supporting enforcement activities, the person within the establishment who will be penalized, etc.—should be detailed in the legislation or ordinance.

In the sections below, we discuss several important themes that emerged from our analysis, and we conclude with a section that addresses the policy implications of our study applicable to both tobacco control initiatives and to an array of other public health measures.

RELATIONSHIP BETWEEN LEGISLATIVE ENACTMENT, IMPLEMENTATION, AND ENFORCEMENT

In conceiving this project, we viewed it as a natural follow-up to our earlier analysis on the political evolution of tobacco control laws (see Jacobson, Wasserman, and Raube, 1993). While the previous work examined the process by which statewide tobacco control laws were enacted—including the roles played by the various stakeholders and the strategies used by tobacco control coalitions and the tobacco industry to frame the legislative debate—during the course of the present project we examined how tobacco control laws are implemented and enforced. In other words, we investigated the question of precisely what happens in states and locales *after* tobacco control laws are enacted. We have realized, however, that the distinction between enactment and implementation/enforcement is an artificial one, and that, in a very real sense, the two are inextricably linked.

Specifically, many of the respondents argued that the enactment process itself—particularly in instances where that process was protracted—served to change attitudes and social norms regarding the importance of tobacco control measures.[1] At least for the clean indoor air measures, these changed social norms paved the way for a smooth implementation process and minimized the need to embark on a vigorous enforcement effort, thus leaving these laws to be primarily self-enforcing. Moreover, as one observer noted, the enactment of tobacco control laws helps shift the balance of power in favor of nonsmokers, which may lead them to speak out in instances where they believe the laws are being violated.

We found that the strength of this relationship weakened somewhat when it came to teen access laws. Here we observed a distinction between statewide laws and local ordinances. Although evidence from compliance checks taken across study sites indicates that a substantial fraction of cigarette vendors all but ignored state laws

[1]Clearly, the extensive enactment of smoking control laws reflects the fact that public opinion and social norms have already changed in favor of additional controls. Nevertheless, we found that at the margin the enactment process created a forum to debate competing viewpoints, which, in turn, often resulted, in convincing one or two city council members to change their attitude and support the measure. It is likely that the council hearings and the attendant media coverage also acted to change the attitudes of members of the community as well.

prohibiting the sale of cigarettes to minors, we noted significant declines in illegal sales rates in locales that had enacted teen access ordinances. It is difficult to attribute such declines to any single element of the ordinance development and implementation process, but we noted that in some of the most successful cases (e.g., Shoreview, Minnesota) the merchants played a key role in crafting the ordinances and in designing merchant education programs.

Apart from the role that the enactment process plays in shaping social norms, it also often has a very concrete effect on implementation and enforcement activities. The absence of specific enforcement provisions in a statewide law or local ordinance can contribute to the failure of the law or ordinance to have its desired effect. For example, several respondents noted that the failure of Tempe, Arizona's vending machine ordinance was due to the fact that the ordinance did not contain any enforcement provisions. Similarly, in New York State, one respondent noted, if

> the coalition had recognized the department of tax and finance's indifference regarding license suspension, [the coalition] would have pushed for different legislation. In New York, licensure came first, and no thought was given to whether and how licensure would be enforced. The 1992 [Youth Access] law built upon the existing licensure structure, thinking that the department of tax and finance would have an incentive to comply. Unfortunately, there are no lists of licensed vendors easily available, resulting in lax enforcement. Therefore, good enforcement is linked to legislation.

EFFECTIVE ENFORCEMENT MECHANISMS

Clean Indoor Air

As we have already mentioned, clean indoor air laws are for the most part self-enforcing in the sense that people are generally made aware of the law through a variety of educational programs and media campaigns, and implicitly agree to comply with its provisions. If an individual smoker or establishment refuses to comply with the law, then an administrative penalty may be imposed on the offending party. That is, a police officer, code officer, or health official may ideally issue a citation that requires the violator to pay a fine—which should increase with the number of violations—or appear in court.

As we have seen in the case of the Austin (Texas) ordinance, requiring city attorneys to file court complaints against violators is both costly and ineffective. Disgruntled merchants, for example, seemed prepared to flagrantly disregard the law knowing that it was unlikely that any such complaints would be filed.

One recommendation for increasing the effectiveness of clean indoor air laws is that criteria for defining or characterizing establishments should be clearly articulated in either the laws themselves or in the accompanying regulations. It is particularly critical to clearly distinguish restaurants from bars, as the latter are often exempt from clean indoor air laws.

Finally, an effort should be made to minimize the number of exceptions to the law, since failure to do so will lead to costly hearings and present tricky enforcement problems. As the number of exceptions grows, the probability of violations appears to increase, as merchants, intentionally or unintentionally, maintain that the law does not apply to their establishments because they fall into an exempt category. Restaurateurs are most likely to complain about complexity. In New York City, for instance, the local anti-tobacco ordinance is quite complex, with exceptions for restaurants under 35 seats and those attached to a bar area. A representative of the restaurant association complained that it was difficult for his members to know whether or not they were in compliance.

Youth Access

Our case study results make it abundantly clear that an ongoing enforcement effort—complete with routine compliance checks—is important for reducing the rate of illegal cigarette sales to minors. Additionally, we found that to be effective, local ordinances must have a graduated penalty structure that starts with a moderate fine for the first offense and escalates in severity with each subsequent offense.

We also believe that licensing cigarette vendors at the local level is a critical ingredient to an effective enforcement program for two reasons. First, as we observed in several Minnesota locales, license fees can be used to finance regular compliance checks, thus making the enforcement effort economically self-sufficient. This, in turn, will ensure its long-run survival. Second, license suspension for varying periods of time, depending on the number of prior offenses, should be an integral component of the ordinance's penalty structure, since even substantial fines may, in some instances, fail to provide a substantial deterrent to illegal sales. For chronic offenders, license revocation should also be an option.

Based on our case studies, we have concluded that penalizing youths for purchasing or possessing cigarettes is not a desirable policy option. Apart from the fact that such laws smack of "blaming the victim," particularly if one believes that cigarette advertising is designed to recruit new, young smokers, they may simply not be cost-effective from a law enforcement perspective. As one senior law enforcement official in Minnesota (which has a state law prohibiting youths from purchasing or possessing tobacco products) remarked, "I can't afford to have my officers sitting in the bushes waiting to catch a kid lighting up." For both economic and philosophical reasons, our interviews revealed that, at least in Minnesota, local law enforcement officials are generally quite reluctant to enforce the law.

ABDICATION OF A STATE STRATEGY BY ANTI-TOBACCO ADVOCATES

To some extent, the lack of commitment that anti-tobacco forces have shown toward implementation and enforcement issues is a reflection of the fact that their resources are being directed to fight preemption attempts at the state level and to enact tobacco control ordinances at the local level. This diversion of resources is the direct result of the tobacco industry's strategy to focus its attention at the state level and, specifically, on a preemption strategy. This strategy has essentially raised the costs faced by anti-tobacco activists to enact, implement, and enforce tobacco control measures by substantially reducing, if not eliminating, the prospects of passing stringent statewide legislation.

As we have detailed elsewhere (see Jacobson, Wasserman, and Raube, 1993), the tobacco industry has historically relied on behind-the-scenes maneuvering to ensure favorable legislative outcomes. Often, this has meant making large campaign contributions to key legislators and employing well-known, in-state lobbyists who enjoy close relationships with influential legislators. This strategy has proven quite successful in blocking the enactment of significant anti-tobacco legislation in many states and in including preemption clauses in others. In fact, it has resulted in an almost total abdication of a statewide strategy on the part of anti-tobacco forces.

The success of the tobacco industry at the state level is illustrated in the case of Texas. Only a few years ago, anti-tobacco forces believed that they had a better than even chance of seeing a stringent clean indoor air bill enacted. Now, however, they, along with their counterparts in many other states (including Arizona and Minnesota), are clearly in a defensive position, where victory is viewed as turning back an industry-sponsored preemption attempt. As one longtime anti-tobacco advocate put it, "Many of us would give up trying to pass a meaningful statewide law if we could be guaranteed that the legislature would never pass a preemption bill."

For now, anti-tobacco advocates in several of the states visited, including Texas and Arizona, have taken the battle to the local level, a far more costly endeavor relative to enacting a statewide bill, but one that faces a far less formidable tobacco industry led opposition. Ultimately, we believe that the local strategy will allow anti-tobacco forces to prevail at the state level, as we have seen in California, and perhaps to a lesser degree in New York State. As the number and strength of local ordinances grows, a "climate of acceptability" develops that, in turn, leads to the development of stringent statewide measures, such as California's AB-13. It should be noted, however, that, as we have seen in California, once statewide legislation was enacted, the number of new local ordinances slowed substantially.

SYMBOLIC STATEMENTS AND CULTURAL CHANGE

Differences in Enforcing and Implementing Clean Indoor Air Regulations and Youth Access Restrictions

Some commentators have hypothesized that the vagueness of most statewide legislation and concomitant limitations in enforcement authority render statewide legislation more of a symbolic statement of intention to control smoking than an easily enforceable mandate. Even when enacted, these laws are subject to legal challenge and are likely to be self-executing rather than susceptible to rigorous enforcement activity. In contrast, local ordinances are likely to be enforced by local authorities who may be more accountable to anti-tobacco coalition pressure (Jacobson, Wasserman, and Raube, 1993; Samuels et al., 1992; Samuels and Glantz, 1991). Our results in this project suggest that these hypotheses are accurate for clean indoor air laws, but not for youth access restrictions.

Most respondents agreed that the clean indoor air acts will be self-executing through community values, but that the prospect of fines and license forfeiture renders youth access restrictions susceptible to enforcement efforts. "People will basically follow the Clean Indoor Air Act, and it is hard to determine what the state would do beyond what it is already doing," noted one observer. For example, it is hard to issue a ticket or citation for smoking—local law enforcement agencies could write citations but are unlikely to do so. This also raises the (unwelcome) specter of the smoking police. In short, neither the state nor the local coalition is engaged in formal activity to enforce clean indoor air regulations.

Part of this response may indicate lowered expectations for implementation and enforcement in this area. As another observer noted,

> The Clean Indoor Air Act is working as expected. You can't legislate this issue—civil norms dominate—and change must be societal. Nevertheless, legislation can stimulate social change, and evolutionary social change is occurring.

That is, clean indoor air laws act as a sentinel that sets new standards of behavior by limiting smoking in public places. Many respondents in New York State noted changes in the cultural environment of the state since our previous interviews, suggesting that the cultural expectation now is not to smoke. Therefore, several respondents argued that no major enforcement effort is needed.

Clean indoor air laws are thus self-executing (or are not executed at all). The same cannot be said for youth access restrictions, which rely heavily on law enforcement to be effective. Repeatedly, our respondents indicated that concomitant cultural changes had not occurred among merchants regarding sales to minors, and that sales to minors would not diminish absent an aggressive enforcement program. This suggests that coalitions and government agencies need to focus their efforts on designing effective strategies to address the barriers to enforcing youth access laws. This is not to suggest that coalitions and enforcement agencies should simply defer to civil norms regarding clean indoor air laws. To the contrary, we discuss below some potential responses coalitions might develop even in the absence of a committed government enforcement program.

Instead, our results indicate that enforcement agencies rely on coalition and individually generated complaints for clean indoor air enforcement but need to be much more aggressive in developing an active compliance strategy to enforce youth access laws. From a policy perspective, our results suggest that government agencies should allocate greater resources to enforcing youth access laws than clean indoor air laws.

On a cautionary note, however, a prominent anti-tobacco advocate argued that kids will still have access to cigarettes, just as they have access to alcohol.

> The answer does not lie strictly in enforcement, although vending machines are susceptible to public policy. The future is not through sales enforcement. A two-pronged approach is needed: a pro-health campaign directed to children and raising the price of cigarettes. Media, public pressure, and price increases are the best strategies.

In a sense, this advocate supported Glantz's (1996) arguments that tobacco control advocates should not focus exclusively on limiting teen access to tobacco products but should concentrate on developing a comprehensive tobacco control agenda.

Scale and Commitment

Our results suggest that scale and commitment are important components of whether tobacco control laws are implemented and enforced. For a variety of obvious reasons, it is feasible to enforce tobacco control laws in smaller communities; in larger cities, there are simply too many vendors to monitor given the available enforcement resources. But even in smaller jurisdictions, enforcement requires political will and commitment. For instance, the Chatauqua County (New York) Health Department (DOH) meets with every major employer regarding their smoking policy. The small scale of the community allows the DOH to operate in a cooperative, nonadversarial manner. Scale alone, however, is not a predictor of enforcement activity. Not all of the smaller jurisdictions in our sample maintain aggressive enforcement activities, and some of the larger cities, including New York and Chicago, have devoted considerable resources to implementation and enforcement efforts.

Our interviews revealed little direct political interference with enforcement and implementation. Even though political concerns have not surfaced, the failure of political officials to allocate sufficient resources to enforcement suggests a general lack of political will and commitment. In this sense, the barriers to enforcement and implementation are largely political.

LESSONS REGARDING COALITION ACTIVITY

Anti-tobacco coalitions remain a central force in tobacco control activities. Although our study was not designed to assess the operation of anti-tobacco coalitions, it appears that coalitions remain dormant regarding enforcement activities and are only somewhat more engaged in implementation, primarily education. We recognize that it is much easier for coalitions to organize around legislation but conclude that sustained coalition enforcement and implementation activity is a necessary component of an effective tobacco control program. Absent pressure from coalitions, state and local agencies are unlikely to mount consistent and comprehensive enforcement efforts.

Enforcement and Implementation

The general deference to state and local agencies to enforce the tobacco control laws makes sense. But coalitions need not abdicate enforcement activities altogether. More important, coalitions may have a comparative advantage in implementation efforts, such as direct contact with merchants and schools and the ability to gain media exposure for grass roots educational campaigns. In addition, coalitions, especially those with a broad and diverse membership, are well-positioned to make the moral arguments in favor of stricter enforcement of both clean indoor air and youth access laws (e.g., merchants who sell cigarettes to children deserve to have their licenses suspended or revoked).

Youth Access. For youth access restrictions, coalitions should be active participants in recruiting underage volunteers for stings. Recruitment is an integral component of a successful enforcement program. Given their community contacts, coalitions are in a better position to recruit a sustainable cadre of volunteers than governmental agencies. Coalitions can also conduct surveys of tobacco use to determine whether active enforcement of youth access restrictions reduces smoking initiation rates among minors.

If youth access restrictions are to become meaningful, greater attention to smoking and its consequences will be required in schools. Yet our interviews suggest great reluctance to treat smoking seriously among schools in most of our sample states. At this point, schools are much more concerned with illicit substances. Some respondents noted safety concerns, while others indicated that teachers do not like the involvement with law enforcement. Overriding these issues is the general attitude that "kids know how easy it is to get cigarettes," so why bother with enforcement.

With their presence in the community, coalitions can bring pressure on school districts and on individual schools to eliminate smoking. For example, although the New York State Pro Kids bill bars smoking on all school grounds, one coalition activist was unable to get her daughter's school principal to convey the no-smoking message to students and to restrict janitors from smoking in the bathrooms. Nor was her school district any more interested. She was persistent and the school finally put up signs and began to address the issue. To the respondent, the importance of the state law is for advocates to be able to say "you must do it."

Another approach is to cooperate with local officials in developing programs that the government alone cannot implement. For instance, the Chatauqua County (New York) Health Department, in conjunction with the local anti-tobacco coalition, has begun an educational "No Proof/No Puffs" campaign targeting cigarette vendors. As another example, the Suffolk County (New York) Health Department is developing a pilot program, as part of the drug-free schools initiative, to identify 70 licensed tobacco vendors. They will receive a mailing from the school district reminding them of the law and asking them to "do the right thing." Then, pairs of students (20 volunteers) will visit the merchants and ask them not to sell to kids and will provide signs. Following this outreach and education campaign, all 70 will be stung. The department of health will ask parents and teachers to talk to any violators.

Clean Indoor Air. Coalitions are probably correct not to allocate considerable resources to enforcing clean indoor air regulations. However, it is important for coalitions to continue to take actions that will reinforce changes in cultural and civil norms that encourage voluntary compliance with tobacco control laws. For example, coalitions can develop and publicize lists of smoke-free restaurants and encourage coalition members to request other restaurants to go smoke free. Likewise, coalitions can generate complaints to enforcement agencies. To our surprise, none of the coalitions in our sample had a strategy for generating complaints. In our view, complaints are important as a measure of how well the laws are working, of the resources the enforcement agencies need to allocate to the program, and to show merchants that they will be held accountable for failure to comply with the law. If coalitions want enforcement agencies to maintain tobacco control as a high priority, it is necessary for them to establish the need. As an example, a person hired for tobacco control compliance in Nassau County (New York) was shifted to other duties because of a diminishing workload.

Many respondents argued that coalitions should focus on educating the community as its top priority. One coalition activist went further, stating that

> The tobacco lobby has framed the post-law issue as 'butt-inskies' (no pun intended) and smoking police. The coalition needs to build a better partnership with [the enforcement agencies] to generate complaints and enforce compliance with the laws. Another response should be to work with restaurants that have supported anti-tobacco laws to show that these laws do not harm business. The coalition needs to get restaurant owners to talk about how business improved. Part of implementation is to develop an offensive strategy, such as using restaurateurs who favor anti-tobacco laws to talk to the public and shape the debate. Right now, the debate is being won by restaurant owners who claim they are losing money.

Thus, coalitions can encourage allies to participate in public campaigns that might blunt the tobacco industry's media efforts to show that anti-tobacco laws are burdensome to small employers. Coalitions can also conduct studies showing the benefits of compliance with tobacco control laws.

Anticipating the Industry Response

It is perhaps gratuitous to note that the tobacco industry will respond in some way to any change in coalition strategy. Thus, it is important for coalitions to anticipate how and why the tobacco industry will alter their approach to obviate the coalitions' efforts. In particular, our interviews suggest that the tobacco industry has been successful in raising the specter of the dreaded smoking police as a way of blunting more aggressive coalition enforcement efforts, at least on the clean indoor air side.

A New York State coalition member engaged in legislative lobbying observed that the tobacco industry's legislative strategy (e.g., preemption) ties up the advocates so that the coalition's legislation, the Healthy Children's Act (which would permit local licensure of tobacco vendors), is languishing. This suggests that a continuing industry legislative assault not only benefits the industry by placing its opponents in a defensive posture legislatively, it also distracts them from their other advocacy goals. Like the ability of the tobacco control movement to distract the industry through many local ordinances, the tobacco industry has a similar strategy of tying up coalition energies and resources at the legislative level.

Developing a Regional Strategy

Our results indicate that only a few sites have developed regional strategies for coalitions to pursue. Such strategies are potentially productive for several reasons. First, regional strategies can address border crossing problems that reduce incentives for individual municipalities to enact and enforce ordinances. Second, there may be enforcement synergies if enforcement officials from contiguous jurisdictions participate in tobacco control enforcement. Third, regional approaches will force various local coalitions to cooperate on enforcement and implementation and to make enforcement a higher coalition priority.

POLICY IMPLICATIONS

The legislative process will continue to be the primary battleground for public health issues ranging from tobacco control to gun control and motorcycle helmets. When considering what compromises to accept to achieve specified legislative goals, public health advocates first need to consider the locus of enforcement responsibility and the sanctions available to the enforcement agency. In general, our results do not augur well for public health measures that depend on state-level enforcement and that are opposed by powerful and politically well-connected interests.

Enforcement is an integral component of effective legislation that should not be discarded or ignored, especially the potential for local license suspension or revocation. As both the literature and our results suggest, legislation and implementation are intertwined. In particular, effective enforcement is linked to legislation that provides specific enforcement mechanisms, such as license removal. Had the New York State coalition recognized the tax and finance department's indifference regarding license suspension, it would have pushed for different legislation. In New York, licensure came first, and no thought was given to whether and how license suspension might be enforced. The 1992 youth access law built upon the existing licensure structure, with the thought that the tax and finance department would have an incentive to comply.

In addition, a complex interplay exists between the process of enacting new legislation and subsequent implementation and enforcement efforts. As a result, public health advocates must use the enactment process as an opportunity to educate both legislators and the public at large on the merits of the proposed legislation. Such educational initiatives may be a necessary precursor to changing attitudes and eventually social norms in favor of the principles embodied in the legislation.

At the same time, the enactment process also provides an opportunity to specify the enforcement mechanisms—including the locus of enforcement,[2] sanctions, and so on—that will be used to ensure compliance with the law. Our results suggest that failure to specify such mechanisms in the legislation will lead to delays in implementing and enforcing the laws as well as to a number of compliance problems. It must be noted, however, that to the extent that the specific public health issue is likely to be self-enforcing, these issues will be less critical.

A second policy implication that can be derived from our findings and applied to a broad set of public health measures is that the burden of implementing and enforcing the laws must be shared between the responsible government agencies and public health advocates. In the current political climate, resource constraints at all levels of government abound. No one can be completely confident that the required resources will be devoted to ensure the effective implementation and enforcement of public health laws, particularly those associated with long-term, chronic phenomena such as smoking. As we have seen in all of our study states, prior to the advent of the Synar Amendment virtually no attempt was made at the state level to enforce laws prohibiting the sale of tobacco products to minors, even though such laws had in many cases been on the books for decades.

Anti-tobacco coalitions, as well as other coalitions that develop to support the adoption of public health measures, should broaden the role that they have historically assumed, which focuses on enacting legislation, to include implementation and enforcement concerns. Upon enacting a significant piece of public health legislation, coalitions should initiate large-scale educational and media campaigns to inform both the affected business interests and the general public about the provisions of the law and what is required of them to comply with it. Coalitions can aid in enforcement efforts by, in the case of teen access laws, for example, recruiting youths to participate in sting operations. Moreover, coalitions can play a central role in collecting and analyzing compliance data and in sharing these data

---

[2]A critical issue concerning the locus of enforcement is whether enforcement authority should be vested in a public health or law enforcement agency. It should be recognized that the latter may have somewhat less of a commitment to tobacco control than public health agencies.

with community leaders and law enforcement officials. Most important, coalitions can become a constant force in pushing state and local enforcement agencies to remove licenses and can put pressure on the legislature and the appropriate enforcement officials to allocate more resources for the effort to implement the latest laws.

A third policy implication of our work centers on the need to include graduated penalty systems into public health legislation. In instances where either no penalty was specified in the law or ordinance or where the penalty appeared to exceed the bounds of reason, we found that, more likely than not, the law would go unenforced. In one case, a city council amended an ordinance to include a graduated penalty structure after it concluded that the local police force was unwilling to cite violators because they believed that the penalty was too harsh. In the case of restricting cigarette sales to minors as well as other public health measures where a policy of licensing vendors of a good or service is viable, we also believe that license suspension and revocation should be included in the penalty structure.

Fourth, a local or regional enforcement strategy appears to be preferable to a state-level one. Many of our respondents noted that state-level enforcement of state laws is often inefficient or ineffective. Typically, at least with respect to tobacco control, local law enforcement officials are well aware of the places in their communities that are engaged in illegal tobacco sales and are prepared to intervene, provided that they have adequate resources at their disposal to do so. In general, local communities have a greater incentive vis-à-vis states to monitor compliance with public health laws. And, as previous studies have shown, the tobacco industry is considerably more powerful at the state, than at the local, level (Jacobson, Wasserman, and Raube, 1993; Samuels and Glantz, 1991; Samuels et al., 1992). Based on our site visits, we believe that local enforcement is a critical ingredient to the success of virtually any tobacco control effort, regardless of whether it revolves around clean indoor air or teen access.

Fifth, both in enacting public health laws and in developing implementation plans, efforts should be made to consolidate implementation and enforcement functions under a single authority. In several study states, responsibility for tobacco control is highly fragmented, which significantly weakens enforcement programs and compromises the objectives of the legislation.

Sixth, despite Glantz's (1996) concerns that the focus on youth access restrictions will impede a more comprehensive anti-tobacco effort, the fact remains that few people choose to begin smoking in their 20s and beyond. Thus, it makes sense to concentrate resources on school-based and other youth programs targeted at reducing smoking initiation rates (Brownson et al., 1995). We now know, for example, that until recently, smoking initiation rates for black youths were far less than for white youths. According to the Centers for Disease Control, that trend has been reversed. What can we learn about why rates for black youths have fluctuated so rapidly? How can those lessons be extrapolated to other groups? If society is serious about preventing sales of alcohol to minors, why not apply the same stringency to prevent the sale of tobacco to minors? We also know that legislators are more inclined to enact anti-tobacco legislation that protects children (Jacobson, Wasserman, and Raube, 1993). For these reasons, a strategy focusing on reducing youth access to cigarettes should remain a primary concern for anti-tobacco advocates.

Appendix A

TEXAS CASE STUDY

INTRODUCTION

Historically, the anti-tobacco forces in Texas have been unsuccessful in passing significant statewide tobacco control legislation—both with respect to clean indoor air and teen access. To a large extent, the failure to enact such legislation stems from the success of the tobacco industry in creating roadblocks in the state's House of Representatives as well as from a general antipathy toward passing legislation that is viewed by many as an attempt to regulate personal behavior (Jacobson, Wasserman, and Raube, 1993). In fact, according to several observers, a series of repeated setbacks in the state legislature has led anti-tobacco activists to virtually abandon their efforts to pass a statewide clean indoor air bill and instead to focus on ensuring that the tobacco industry fails to have legislation enacted that would preempt local tobacco control initiatives. Interestingly, while the prospects for passage of a statewide clean indoor air act appear dim, a number of interviewees held out the possibility that a teen access bill might pass the legislature.

The failure to enact a statewide tobacco control bill has left many proponents of tougher smoking laws with a deep sense of cynicism. One observer noted that

> You have to be very suspicious of any [tobacco control] law that's passed on the state level. Many of us would give up trying to pass a meaningful statewide law if we could be guaranteed that the legislature would never pass a preemption bill.

At the same time, the series of successive losses at the state level has caused the anti-tobacco coalition to change its overall strategy and shift attention to community outreach activities, including distributing "advocacy packets" and sample tobacco control ordinances, conducting health fairs, and working with local health educators to ensure that tobacco control remains high on their agendas. An integral component of this new strategy is encouraging local communities to pass ordinances aimed at both restricting smoking in public places and limiting teenagers' access to cigarettes.

The picture, however, is considerably brighter on the local level, where Texas has witnessed the passage of stringent anti-tobacco ordinances in nearly half of the state's 200 largest cities (Texas Department of Health, 1991). As one observer pointed out, "Texas has been relatively successful at picking away at the problem on the local level." To gain insight into how local ordinances have been implemented and enforced, we conducted site visits to two Texas cities (Austin and Arlington) that have recently enacted anti-tobacco ordinances. The two sites were selected after consulting with several individuals who are active in the state's tobacco control movement.

Before describing the experiences of these two communities with respect to tobacco control, we first address the role that the state has played in implementing and enforcing tobacco control laws.

STATE-LEVEL EFFORTS TO IMPLEMENT AND ENFORCE TOBACCO CONTROL LAWS

The absence of any stringent statewide tobacco control laws in Texas obviates the need for a rigorous implementation and/or enforcement effort. In fact, none of the interviewees mentioned the existence of any enforcement activities aimed at ensuring compliance with the state's rather minimal clean indoor air laws. These laws essentially require only that smoking be restricted to designated areas in indoor theaters, libraries, museums, public transportation, and hospitals, and that students be prohibited from smoking at any school-related functions on or off school property (Coalition on Smoking OR Health, 1993).

Texas has, however, taken an active role in enforcing the law that prohibits the sale of cigarettes to minors under the age of 18. To a large extent, the activism is in response to the requirements of the Synar Amendment, which mandates that states demonstrate ongoing reductions in teen smoking rates or risk losing a portion of their block grants for alcohol and drug abuse prevention and treatment programs.

The Texas Commission on Alcohol and Drug Abuse (TCADA) has voluntarily assumed responsibility for ensuring that the state complies with the requirements imposed by Synar because it risked losing just under nine million dollars in federal block grants during the first year of Synar's implementation. In an effort to reduce tobacco use among the state's youth, TCADA contracted with the Texas DARE[1] Institute to train over 650 DARE officers on the health effects of tobacco use, state law governing the sale of tobacco to minors, and methods for conducting compliance checks and educating tobacco retailers.

Additionally, to monitor the incidence of tobacco sales to minors, TCADA contracted for the conduct of annual inspections and the generation of statewide estimates of the illegal sales rate. The baseline survey, conducted in mid-1994, found that the illegal purchase rate for over-the-counter sales was 56 percent, while the corresponding rate for vending machine sales hit 93 percent. With this monitoring mechanism in place, and a cadre of trained law enforcement officials, TCADA hopes to demonstrate a decline in illegal purchases in the years ahead. The extent to which these hopes are realized, as well as whether any such decline translates into reductions in youth tobacco use, remains unclear.

In addition to the activities conducted by TCADA, the Texas Department of Health maintains a network of regional tobacco education and prevention specialists who are charged with training volunteers, forming local tobacco control coalitions, educating retailers, conducting compliance inspections, and providing other forms of technical assistance, including offering expert testimony at city council hearings on tobacco control ordinances.

---

[1] DARE stands for Drug Abuse Resistance Education.

LOCAL EFFORTS TO IMPLEMENT AND ENFORCE TOBACCO CONTROL LAWS

The absence of statewide tobacco control legislation in Texas necessarily implies that the state has relatively little to offer by way of insight into implementation and enforcement issues. In contrast, a large number of local communities throughout the state have passed and implemented both clean indoor air and teen access ordinances. As noted above, we selected two communities, Austin and Arlington, for study. For very different reasons, and as described below, these two sites provide important lessons with respect to both implementation and enforcement.

Austin

In early 1994, the City of Austin passed an ordinance restricting smoking in public places that substantially strengthened a series of previous ordinances. In particular, the focus of the ordinance was on further restricting smoking in restaurants. The new ordinance is exceedingly complex: Its provisions vary by time of day, type of dining establishment, and age of facility. For example, while smoking is generally not permitted in dining areas of existing restaurants, it is permitted in these areas if (1) it is between the hours of 10:00 p.m. and 6:00 a.m. or if the kitchen is closed and dining service has been discontinued; (2) the areas reserved for smoking is proportionate to the number of patrons requesting that they be seated in a smoking area; and (3) on or before March 15, 1996, the smoking area has a separate heating, ventilation, and air conditioning (HVAC) system. Moreover, smoking is permitted in "special separate dining areas" of restaurants provided that such areas are enclosed on all sides or are enclosed on three sides with solid walls and separated from nonsmoking areas on the fourth side by at least 15 feet and have separate HVAC systems. Again, these separate dining areas must be in proportion in size to the number of patrons who normally request seating in a smoking area.

The ordinance is vague in a number of key areas. For instance, it fails to specify precisely what constitutes a separate HVAC system. Interestingly, this ambiguity is viewed by many stakeholders on both sides of the issue to work in their favor. Supporters of the ordinance view it as a backdoor way of achieving a complete ban on restaurant smoking, reasoning that most restaurants would be unwilling to incur the costs associated with retrofitting their facilities with effective, well-engineered ventilation systems, implicitly assuming that such systems are what is required by the ordinance. Opponents of the ordinance, on the other hand, believe that the ambiguous provision was intended to ensure minimal compliance costs. In their minds, an open window will do.

A second source of ambiguity contained in the ordinance is a provision that exempts “live music venues,” which are defined simply as establishments where live music is performed at least three days per week and a cover charge is collected at least two days per week. It does, however, require that these establishments offer at least 25 percent nonsmoking shows of a minimum of two hours in duration. This provision of the ordinance is perceived as a major loophole.

The Austin-Travis County Health and Human Services Department’s Environmental Health Services Division is charged with enforcing the ordinance. The enforcement system is essentially a complaint-driven one, since the division has only one FTE assigned to enforce the ordinance, which covers approximately 4,000 restaurants. While the division has not attempted to measure compliance in any systematic fashion, it is the staff’s perception that the vast majority of the establishments are complying with the ordinance. The division received 228 complaints for the remainder of the fiscal year during which the ordinance was passed (approximately nine months). The enforcement guidelines developed by the division stipulate that following a complaint, the alleged violator will be issued a letter informing him or her that a complaint has been received and that they have 10 days to correct the problem. A follow-up inspection is made, and if the establishment is found to be in violation of the ordinance, then a legal notice, or citation, is issued specifying that the owner or person responsible for the establishment has 10 days to correct the problem. A second follow-up inspection is made after 10 days have elapsed, and if the establishment is still found to be in violation, then the case is referred to a prosecuting attorney who then files a complaint against the violator in municipal court. To date, only two such case have been brought, neither of which resulted in a conviction. It is uncertain, however, whether this small number of cases is reflective of a high level of compliance with the ordinance or of the notion that costs of prosecuting such cases are high relative to the expected benefits of pursuing this type of strategy. A number of observers suggested that an enforcement system that would allow police or code officers to issue a citation that carries a moderate fine would be more effective.

The Environmental Health Services Division is virtually the only organizational entity that is involved with enforcing the ordinance. It also assumed a major role in educating affected businesses about the ordinance's provision by having its community safety officers distribute flyers and by developing a guidelines document. Members of the local coalition, disappointed with their inability to achieve a total smoking ban in restaurants, have moved on to other issues, in particular youth access. Some coalition members indicated that playing a role in the enforcement effort may threaten their economic interests. As one voluntary association staffer put it, "We don't want to be seen as having a front-line role in the compliance effort. As a fundraising organization, we don't want to create the impression that we're out to get the retailers."

For the most part, interviewees reported that restaurant owners are complying with the ordinance, but, again, there have been no rigorous evaluations of the ordinance to support their assertions. One observer added that compliance with the ordinance was high because the economy in Austin was "booming." He cautioned, however, that "if the economy goes down, the smoking ordinance would come back up [in the City Council]." This sentiment was echoed by a second interviewee who indicated that economic arguments resonated among council members.

Pockets of resistance to the ordinance can still be found in some quarters. When asked about his plans for complying with the ordinance, one restaurateur nodded in the direction of a group of distant smokers and said "we're out of compliance now and I don't expect to do much to change that." After noting that the ordinance was due to "a national fad brought on by Clinton," a second interviewee stated that while "locals are willing to comply as best they can on a partial ban, we'd fight like hell to oppose a total ban."

Arlington

By almost all accounts, Arlington, Texas, represents a textbook case in how to implement, enforce, and, in many respects, enact a stringent tobacco control ordinance. While the enactment phase of the process was, to be sure, contentious, it demonstrated that a well-orchestrated and executed incrementalist strategy on the part of tobacco control proponents can succeed in overcoming significant obstacles posed by opponents of regulation. A concerted effort was made by the ordinance's proponents—both those on and off the city council—to rely on scientific evidence to further their cause. For instance, they calculated that while only 10 to 15 residents were victims of homicide each year, extrapolating downward from national estimates, they found that between 58 and 62 residents died from environmental tobacco smoke (ETS). Moreover, the results of a nonbinding referendum held in 1991 to measure the degree of support for strengthening the city's ordinance indicated that 73 percent of voters were in favor of additional controls in the workplace, and the same majority favored a prohibition on smoking in all indoor places open to the general public.

Passed in January of 1994 as one of a series of amendments to a tobacco control ordinance that has been evolving since its inception in 1985, the current Arlington ordinance bans or severely restricts smoking in a broad array of public places. Such places include, but are not limited to, schools, libraries, health care facilities, indoor or outdoor service lines, retail establishments, workplaces, and eating establishments. In several of these places, smoking is permitted in physically separated designated areas provided that the owner has installed a ventilation system. In contrast to the Austin ordinance, the ventilation system's specifications were clearly defined. For instance, the system can serve no other area, no return air is allowed from the smoking area, the air has to be exhausted to the outside, and the exhaust from the room has to be ventilated at the rate of four exchanges per hour. Moreover, with respect to eating establishments, no more than 30 percent of the total available floor space can be reserved for smoking (Doegey and Barber, 1994). These requirements have led many Arlington-area restaurants to institute smoking bans.

The ordinance is enforced by Arlington's health department, which maintains a field staff of six full-time inspectors to cover the city's restaurants (which number close to 700), day care centers, and swimming pools. Soon after the ordinance was passed, the inspectors carried out a comprehensive set of compliance checks in which they distributed signs to be posted, notices that delineated the contents of the ordinance, and educational materials on precisely what constituted acceptable compliance standards. Once the initial round of inspections was conducted, the system has slowly transformed itself into being essentially complaint driven.

Typically, when a complaint is received regarding a workplace, the health department issues a letter that notifies the employer that a complaint has been filed and that reviews the relevant provisions of the ordinance. If the complainant persists, then the health department visits the site and issues a citation. The fine is set by the municipal court but is generally \$175–\$200. In the case of restaurants, a site visit is generally conducted soon after the complaint is filed. At the inspector's discretion, either a notice informing the owner that a complaint has been filed alleging that his or her establishment is in violation of the ordinance or a citation is issued on the spot. Health department staff reported that they issue only a handful of citations to restaurants and workplaces each month. Moreover, they noted that the bulk of the complaints received were from members of a local anti-tobacco advocacy organization whose director was described by one staffer as a "one-man smoking police force."

The overwhelming majority of interviewees suggested that the ordinance has been widely accepted by restaurateurs, employers, and the public at large and that compliance is quite high. Several noted the extent to which business owners' attitudes toward the ordinance have evolved over time. That is, while opposition to the ordinance in some quarters, particularly restaurants, was initially high, over time virtually all affected businesses have come to accept it, if not willingly embrace it. As a senior city official succinctly put it, the "smoking regulation is working and widely accepted." A second observer stated that implementing smoking regulations was like "putting traffic lights on streets where there were none before—people quickly forget what life was like before the lights were installed."

Perhaps most tellingly, in commenting on a bill introduced in the state legislature that would preempt several key provisions of the Arlington ordinance, the head of the Arlington Restaurant Association, who had vociferously opposed the ordinance's enactment, was quoted in the *Fort Worth Star-Telegram* almost a year after its passage as saying that although he generally supported the notion of a statewide bill he had no desire to see the Arlington ordinance supplanted. "Everyone worked hard to get a win-win situation," he said, "and it worked out okay." Other interviewees opined that smoking regulation was a local matter that had to be responsive to the particular needs and demands of each community. In reference to the state preemption bill, one said simply that he wished that the legislators would "leave them the hell alone and adjourn."

SUMMARY AND CONCLUSIONS

The absence of significant tobacco control legislation at the state level—save a prohibition of the sale of cigarettes to minors—leaves issues related to state-level implementation and enforcement to be of little more than academic interest. While the state has made some effort to comply with the requirements of the Synar Amendment to preserve their alcohol and drug abuse block grants, no state-level tobacco control initiative is, or has been, in the offing. In fact, the sense of optimism that we earlier observed on the part of antitobacco advocates in the state has all but vanished (Jacobson, Wasserman, and Raube, 1993), and such advocates instead have lowered their hopes and expectations considerably. Now, victory is seen as successfully turning back tobacco industry–sponsored efforts to preempt local ordinances.

At the same time, staff from the health department and other state-level organizations have actively supported local initiatives to both restrict teen access to cigarettes and limit smoking in public places. Over the last decade, many locales have successfully enacted ordinances in both of these areas; but implementation and enforcement efforts have met with more mixed success.

As we have seen, the vague and complex provisions of the Austin ordinance have proven somewhat problematic. Because no formal compliance studies have been undertaken, we are unable to report the precise extent to which affected businesses obey the law. Although anecdotal evidence indicates that compliance is generally high, instances of noncompliance abound and almost all observers are in agreement that the law has gaping holes. Moreover, disgruntled merchants are willing to risk being cited for noncompliance knowing that it is unlikely that a court action will actually be brought against them.

However, the case of Arlington illustrates that it is possible to successfully enact, implement, and enforce a rather stringent local ordinance, which was ultimately found to enjoy broad public support, even among some of its initial opponents. A number of interviewees attributed the ordinance's success to the incrementalist approach adopted by the city council, the fact that there were a number of city council people around to "carry the torch," the public's solid support for additional controls, and the intelligence of spokespeople on both sides of the issue.

The Roles of Key Stakeholders

Our results relating to the roles of two key stakeholders in the tobacco control process, namely the state's anti-tobacco coalition and the tobacco industry, were remarkably consistent across the sites visited. For example, we found that the members of the statewide coalition and the coalition that was formed around the Austin ordinance[2] played a minor role in the implementation and enforcement process, limiting their activities primarily to distributing educational materials to those affected. As noted previously, to some extent the voluntary health associations made a conscious effort to distance themselves from enforcement issues, fearing that their involvement in this area might threaten their ability to raise funds in their communities. In general, the coalition members believed that enforcement, in particular, and to a lesser extent implementation, should be largely left to state or local government agencies. In addition, the enactment phase of the process was generally viewed as "sexier" in comparison with implementation and enforcement issues, and a

[2] There is no formal local coalition in the Arlington area. Regional staff from the state department of health and the major voluntary health associations, however, frequently testified in support of amendments to the ordinance before the Arlington city council.

tangible product (i.e., a local ordinance or a piece of statewide legislation) resulted from their efforts. The attitude of many coalition members was simply that once a new ordinance or bill was in hand, it was time to move on to the next issue.

In many respects, this attitude was also reflective of the role assumed by the tobacco industry, which, for the most part, "picked up and left town," in the words of one observer, after the ordinance was passed. According to many interviewees in Austin, Arlington, and at the state level, the industry's strategy was essentially to do everything they could to thwart passage of additional anti-tobacco laws—by attempting to organize smokers at the grass roots level into various "smokers' rights groups" and by backing or even creating surrogate organizations such as local restaurant and other merchant associations that could testify against local ordinances—but in the event that they were unsuccessful they simply went on to oppose legislation in other cities. In other words, the industry did not appear to any interviewees in either of the local sites to vigorously impede implementation and enforcement activities once an ordinance was passed.

It is important to note, however, that the industry does not fail to miss an opportunity at the state level to have a local ordinance overturned. For example, it is no coincidence that the preemption bill introduced into the state legislature in March of 1995 would have superseded all local ordinances that took effect after January 1, 1994: the most recent amendments to the Arlington ordinance took effect a mere month later.

Barriers

A number of significant barriers exist at the state level that undermine or impede effective enforcement of the state's law prohibiting the sale of cigarettes to minors. To begin with, the legislature has not assigned responsibility for tobacco control to any state agency. As noted previously, TCADA assumed responsibility for implementing the requirements of the Synar Amendment because it had the most at stake from an economic point of view. While TCADA has made grants to other agencies to conduct compliance surveys, train DARE officers, and so on, the fact remains that there are no dedicated state tobacco control enforcement staff.

A second barrier is that local police forces have not made tobacco law enforcement a high priority. In fact, according to some accounts, even many of the DARE officers failed to embrace the importance of tobacco control and instead focused their educational programs on the hazards associated with alcohol and illicit drugs. As one senior state official put it, "the police are the biggest barrier to effective enforcement because they don't believe that [tobacco control] is an important issue."

Third, and perhaps most disconcerting, proponents of tobacco control in the state appear to have become apathetic. That is, in the face of repeated setbacks in their quest to pass significant statewide legislation and in the face of the hegemony that the tobacco industry currently exercises and enjoys, several interviewees reported that they have had difficulty generating and sustaining interest in implementing and enforcing whatever laws are presently on the books. One of the values of sting operations, one respondent pointed out, was that such operations were a powerful way to mobilize interest in tobacco control.

At the local level, the main barrier appears to be resource constraints. As a result, in both Austin and Arlington, enforcement is largely complaint-driven, and no systematic inspections are carried out, for instance, by code officers. Even in the absence of resource constraints, however, it is difficult to imagine that it would be cost-beneficial to conduct a rigorous series of inspections on a regular basis. First, as described previously, compliance with the ordinances in the two cities is generally felt to be quite high, although more so in Arlington than in Austin. Second, and perhaps more important, it is likely that stringent enforcement efforts may provoke a backlash at the state level. That is, if the tobacco industry's fabricated image of a "smoking police" is in some sense realized, then passage of a state bill that preempts local ordinances seems all the more likely. As one interviewee summed it up, "If you get greedy, you'll lose."

Appendix B

ARIZONA CASE STUDY

INTRODUCTION

Tobacco control, as practiced in Arizona, is primarily a local affair. Despite repeated attempts on the part of anti-tobacco advocates and the state's tobacco control coalition, the state has failed to enact any stringent tobacco control laws. That is, while the state prohibits the sale of cigarettes to minor, it regulates smoking in only a handful of public places such as elevators, buses, schools, and health care institutions. Moreover, in the view of many observers, the prospects for passing a significant statewide bill remain bleak.

Nevertheless, for a number of reasons, the case of Arizona remains an interesting one from a tobacco control perspective. To begin with, the state's coalition, which was filled with internal strife only a few short years ago, played an instrumental role in passing a 1994 ballot initiative that raised the state's cigarette excise tax by 40 cents per pack. Second, the state continues to provide striking examples of how local communities can enact and implement a broad array of tobacco control measures. And third, as described below, through its Synar Amendment–related activities and other initiatives, the state has generated quantitative data on several key tobacco control issues.

STATE-LEVEL EFFORTS TO IMPLEMENT AND ENFORCE SMOKING CONTROL LAWS

Until recently, the dearth of substantial statewide tobacco control legislation in Arizona meant that the department of health services was generally relegated to sponsoring tobacco control educational programs, coordinating the efforts of the statewide coalition, and providing technical assistance to locales and organizations interested in reducing the use of tobacco throughout the state. Moreover, the absence of statewide legislation is symptomatic of the general unwillingness of state legislators and other officials to push for a statewide bill, reasoning that matters related to tobacco control are best left to local communities to decide. One tobacco control advocate indicated that there were enormous political barriers to surmount before a statewide bill, particularly one concerned with clean indoor air, could be passed. She reported that the pro-business bias of many legislators makes it unlikely that they will support legislation that requires businesses to restrict smoking in the workplace and so on and noted that "you will lose some of the folks you get to support kids' [smoking] issues when you start telling businesses what they can and can't do."

With the advent of the Synar Amendment, and its requirement that states demonstrate a good faith effort to reduce tobacco use by teenagers through "sting operations" and other methods, the department of health services stepped up its tobacco control efforts to ensure the preservation of block grant funds.

Specifically, the department of health services' response to Synar was to initiate a set of pilot projects throughout the state aimed at reducing youth access. Through a competitive bidding process, the department selected three cities to receive awards of approximately $30,000 each: Tempe, Flagstaff, and Tucson. To participate in the program, each site was required to (1) conduct three rounds of unannounced inspections of tobacco vendors; (2) engage in a series of activities, such as merchant education programs and media campaigns that were intended to reduce illegal sales to minors; and (3) field pre- and post-intervention surveys of 10th graders to measure their use of, and access to, tobacco products (Arizona Department of Health Services, 1995). The baseline "sting operations" were conducted between April and June 1994, with the two follow-up inspections occurring in November 1994 and January 1995. The youth surveys were administered in May/June 1994, which was prior to any interventions, and November 1994.

The pilot projects' results were mixed. As shown in Table B.1, two of the three sites, Tempe and Flagstaff, achieved significant reductions in the rate of illegal sales to minors between the baseline "sting operation" and the second follow-up. (In the case of Flagstaff, the lowest illegal sales rate was actually observed during the first follow-up.) Note that while the rate of illegal sales in Tucson increased over the baseline—which was quite low in comparison with the other sites—in each of the two follow-up years, the final illegal sales rate for that city was comparable to the other two cities.

With respect to changes in the prevalence of teenage smoking, the results were not encouraging. As shown in Table B.2, although the prevalence of smoking among 10th graders in Flagstaff declined by two percentage points after initiation of the intervention, the corresponding rates for Tempe and Tucson increased by two percentage points and five percentage points, respectively.

Table B.1

Rate of Illegal Sales of Tobacco to Minors in Arizona Cities

Community	Baseline	First Follow-up	Second Follow-up
Flagstaff	.62	.24	.32
Tempe	.65	.62	.27
Tucson	.28	.37	.30

SOURCE: Arizona Department of Health Services, 1995.

Table B.2

Smoking Prevalence Rates Among 10th Graders in Arizona Cities (in percentage)

	Flagstaff	Tempe	Tucson
Pre-intervention	41	24	20
Post-intervention	39	26	25

SOURCE: Arizona Department of Health Services, 1995.

Taken together, the two tables illustrate an important point: Demonstrated reductions in illegal sales rates to minors may not affect minors' cigarette consumption. Take, for example, the case of Tempe. Although the illegal sales rate dropped dramatically in that city between the baseline inspection and the second follow-up, the prevalence rate increased by two percentage points. One possible explanation for these seemingly inconsistent results is simply that the inspections served to concentrate sales to minors in a smaller number of stores. Alternatively, minors in Tempe may simply be choosing to buy cigarettes in a neighboring city, such as Mesa or Phoenix, that has not yet cracked down on vendors.

LOCAL EFFORTS TO IMPLEMENT AND ENFORCE SMOKING CONTROL LAWS

After consulting with several tobacco control experts in the state, we focused our local site visits on two cities, Tempe and Flagstaff. As indicated above, both of these cities were selected to participate in the Synar-related pilot project. Furthermore, both have passed other ordinances that make them interesting candidates for study. Tempe passed a vending machine ordinance that subsequently met with limited success, while Flagstaff enacted a clean indoor air ordinance that severely restricts smoking in restaurants and that appears to have been effectively implemented and accepted by both restaurant establishments and the public at large.

In addition to these sites, we conducted a series of less extensive interviews in two other communities—Scottsdale and Cottonwood—the results of which add further insights into how local tobacco control measures have been implemented and enforced.

Tempe

Pilot Project. The City of Tempe took what may be termed a "stick" approach toward the pilot project. Directed by staff from the city attorney's office, the Tempe pilot project included a media campaign, a merchant education program, and an enforcement component. The media campaign essentially relied on the distribution of materials to the press (including press releases, fact sheets, etc.) and a series of radio and television public service announcements. The merchant education program involved the distribution of a guide on methods of preventing cigarette sales to minors and several follow-up letters on the results of the unannounced inspections.

As indicated in Table B.1, these activities had only a marginal impact between the baseline inspections and the first follow-ups. Thus, prior to the second round of follow-up inspections, the city stepped up the pressure on vendors considerably by notifying all vendors who failed the first two inspections that a third round was planned and that if they failed again they would be cited. During the second set of follow-up inspections, a Tempe police officer accompanied the volunteers conducting the inspections to 10 locations, all of which had failed the first two rounds, and issued eight citations. It is interesting to note that this "get tough" approach indeed had an impact, as evidenced in Table B.1, at least in the short run. One city official noted that the key to long-run decreases in illegal sales rates was direct and continuous contact with the vendors and regular compliance checks.

Vending Machine Ordinance. Tempe's experience with its vending machine ordinance, which became effective in early 1994, is a substantial source of frustration for many of the city's tobacco control advocates. The ordinance, which was crafted as a compromise between council members who favored an outright ban and those who preferred to take no action whatsoever, required the installation of control devices on all vending machines and that the machines be placed in such a manner so as to be directly visible, when operated, by either the owner of the establishment or his or her employee. The ordinance does not contain any specific enforcement provisions, although violators may receive fines of up to $2,500 per day of non-compliance or a prison term of up to six months according to the general penalty provision of the Tempe city code.

The consensus view among both city officials and anti-tobacco advocates is that the ordinance has been an abject failure. A series of inspections of the city's vending machines (which are estimated to number around 20) revealed that only one machine was in compliance with the ordinance approximately six months after it was enacted. Several observers found these results to be not in the least bit surprising. One city council member commented that "the compromise [on the ordinance] was so labor intensive that I knew that it would fail." In addition, he in effect blamed the ordinance's failure on the lack of a strong implementation plan, noting that with reference to tobacco control laws, in general, "Sometimes the message doesn't get out, and in the case of the vending machine ordinance, the message *never* got out once the compromise was reached and the owners of the machines just never did what they said they were going to do." Another interviewee noted simply that the ordinance "doesn't work because it's not a good ordinance, and if there's not a significant enforcement threat, people are not going to comply."

After some negative publicity about their lack of effectiveness in enforcing the ordinance (Natale, 1994), city officials started scrambling. Letters were sent to all vendors who were not complying with the law that additional inspections would be carried out and citations issued. Furthermore, several respondents noted that the poor compliance record on the part of vending machine owners increases the likelihood that an ordinance banning the sale of cigarettes through vending machines would be passed in the not-too-distant future.

Flagstaff

Pilot Project. In contrast to Tempe, which initially took a relatively hands-off, and perhaps even weak, approach toward reducing the illegal sales rate before cracking the whip on recalcitrant vendors, Flagstaff engaged in a more cooperative approach with vendors from the start. Responsibility for implementing the pilot project was vested with the Coconino County Department of Public Health, as opposed to Tempe's decision to vest such authority with the city attorney.

Similar to Tempe, the Flagstaff project included community outreach (i.e., a media campaign and other activities) and merchant education components. Moreover, in an attempt to broaden the base of support for the project in the community, the department of public health created the Youth Access Project Coalition, which included representatives from the city's youth commission, police department, administration, school district, and Citizens Against Substance Abuse, as well as the department (Coconino County Department of Public Health, 1995).

The merchant education component of the intervention, which a number of observers believe was key to the project's success, was decidedly different than the approach taken in Tempe. Specifically, in addition to distributing education packets to vendors that included stickers for the front doors and cash registers, flyers for employees describing how to comply with the law, and a letter from the chief of police, a group meeting was held with vendors to discuss how the package could be used and what steps should be taken to ensure compliance with the state's law governing sales of tobacco products to minors. In a demonstration of their commitment to make face-to-face contact with each of the vendors—and perhaps to display the seriousness with which they intended to implement the enforcement component of the project—a representative from the police department met individually with each of the vendors who did not attend the group meeting.

The approach taken by the department of public health, which, again, focused on community outreach and a "personalized" vendor education program, produced rather impressive results in short order, as the rate of illegal sales dropped from a baseline value of 62 percent to just 24 percent at the first follow-up. (Subsequently, the rate increased somewhat to 32 percent.)

Restaurant Ordinance. Apart from its involvement in the state-sponsored pilot project, Flagstaff also enacted and implemented one of the nation's toughest restaurant ordinances. The initial ordinance prohibiting smoking in restaurants was passed by the city council in 1991. A year later, however, opponents of the ordinance garnered enough votes in the council to have it repealed. In turn, a handful of anti-tobacco activists succeeded in having a referendum passed in November of 1992 that reinstated the ban by a 57 to 43 percent margin.

As is the case with most local tobacco control ordinances, the method of enforcement adopted by Flagstaff is a complaint-driven one. Complaints are submitted to the city's community development agency, which then issues a letter to the alleged violator indicating that a complaint has been received and that the restaurant must comply with the ordinance. If a second complaint is received, the local police would issue a citation. Yet, according to a city official, no restaurants have ever been cited or prosecuted for violating the ordinance.

The results of a survey taken of 34 area restaurants (which represents a random sample of approximately 25 percent of all Flagstaff restaurants) indicated that the ordinance has not proven to be especially burdensome to restaurant owners. For example, 94 percent of the respondents reported that the ordinance was either "easy to enforce" or "very easy to enforce." In addition, and perhaps more important, after the ordinance had been in effect for 15 months, nearly 68 percent of the respondents maintained that the ordinance either increased or had no effect on their respective businesses (Sciacca, 1996). The latter survey results are supported by a recent analysis of Flagstaff restaurant sales data. According to the results of that study—which examined changes over time in the ratio of total restaurant sales to total retail sales in Flagstaff and compared those ratios with those found in other cities throughout the state—there is no evidence that the Flagstaff restaurant ordinance had any adverse effects on restaurant sales (Sciacca, Ratliff, and Pappas, 1996).

The only substantive issue to emerge in an otherwise smooth implementation and enforcement process concerns the provision of the ordinance that exempts bars. Because it is at times difficult to determine whether a particular establishment should be characterized as a bar or restaurant and because the ordinance provides a clear incentive for establishments that serve both food and alcoholic beverage to argue that they are in fact bars, the city drafted administrative regulations that address the issue. These regulations state that if gross revenues from the sale of alcoholic beverages equal or exceed gross sales from food, then the establishment will be considered a bar. During the first 18 months of the ordinance's implementation, the city held hearings to determine the status of five establishments and found that only one should properly be considered a bar.

Other Sites

As indicated earlier, less extensive sets of interviews were held at two additional sites: Scottsdale and Cottonwood. Scottsdale enacted a 1994 ordinance that prohibited the sale of cigarettes through vending machines. Cottonwood, however, passed a referendum in late 1993 that prohibited smoking in all public places except restaurants, bars, and bowling alleys.

The Scottsdale experience is noteworthy because it contrasts sharply with the Tempe vending machine ordinance, which required the installation of control, or locking, devices on all vending machines. As described above, we found that the Tempe ordinance was almost completely disregarded. The simplicity of the Scottsdale ordinance, however, meant only a trivial enforcement effort. Upon passage of the ordinance, the city mailed letters to all affected businesses informing them that cigarette vending machines were prohibited by law. The follow-up to the letters was characterized by one interviewee as "friendly enforcement" in which the police issued only two warnings to establishments that had vending machines on their premises. The respondent added that "the ordinance was passed and virtually everyone complied."

Interviewees credited the success of the ordinance to the fact that it enjoyed widespread public support, that a local coalition of voluntary health associations and anti-tobacco advocacy groups supplied critical information during the enactment process, and that all affected business were contacted once the ordinance was passed and informed about their obligation to remove the vending machines.

Cottonwood provides an illustration of how a town of approximately 6,000 people can enact, implement, and enforce a stringent tobacco control law. There, according to several observers, a substantial grassroots effort was undertaken to ensure the referendum's passage. (One interviewee suggested that the sizable Mormon community in the area was largely responsible for the referendum's success.) The case of Cottonwood is particularly interesting because it shows how the enactment process—in this instance the referendum—is often a key ingredient to the subsequent enforcement process. As one observer stated, "Enforcement isn't the issue; the issue is to tell smokers that their behavior is offensive to other people." In other words, the enactment process may provide an important catalyst for changing social norms.

SUMMARY AND CONCLUSIONS

The sites selected for study in Arizona represent a small but rich collection of examples of how state and local tobacco control laws are implemented and enforced. Additionally, it is one of the few states visited during the course of the project that produced some quantitative data on important study issues.

Arizona's experiences with tobacco control laws have produced their share of successes and failures. For example, as we have seen, the state's approach for complying with the requirements of the Synar Amendment, at least initially, relied on a series of pilot projects that produced mixed, if not somewhat discouraging, results. And while the City of Tempe's vending machine ordinance was all but ignored by vendors, a number of the local ordinances passed should be considered resounding successes from a tobacco control perspective, including the Flagstaff restaurant ordinance and the Scottsdale vending machine ban. Despite differences in the success of these laws, the sites studied showed some remarkable consistencies with respect to roles that some of the key stakeholders played in the implementation and enforcement process as well as to the barriers that tobacco control proponents confronted.

The Roles of Key Stakeholders

At both the state and local levels, we found that while a myriad of organizations played important roles in enacting tobacco control laws, government agencies played the central, if not the exclusive, role in implementation and enforcement efforts. One member of the statewide tobacco control coalition put it succinctly saying that "the main mission of the coalition is enactment." From time to time we observed that while a number of the anti-tobacco advocacy groups paid attention to enforcement concerns—by reporting violations, participating in compliance checks, and monitoring violation hearings—the voluntary health associations and the state and local medical societies were particularly quiescent with respect to enforcement. It should be pointed out, however, that while we did not find organized medicine to be especially active in the tobacco control policymaking arena, individual physicians made important contributions to enacting, and to a lesser degree, implementing tobacco control laws. In Cottonwood, for example, two physicians were almost completely responsible for ensuring passage of the referendum.

Additionally, we were surprised to find that the tobacco industry's representatives confined their most strenuous opposition efforts to the state level, where they made repeated attempts to have preemption legislation introduced. Interestingly, while they maintained at least some presence in each of the locales, they conducted themselves, for the most part, in a rather low-key manner, limiting the bulk of their activities during the enactment phase of the process to providing financial support to front groups (e.g., restaurant and merchant associations that virtually sprung up overnight once an ordinance was introduced) and writing periodic letters to the editors of local newspapers complaining about the burdens of the ordinances, as they perceived them. In Flagstaff, the tobacco industry's role in the entire ordinance development and implementation process was described by one observer as "subdued." A second interviewee noted that "all of the gloom and doom predictions [about how the industry's activities would derail the enactment process] didn't materialize." Although the industry vocalized its opposition to the Flagstaff ordinance while it was under debate, and during the subsequent referendum movement, industry representatives "disappeared entirely once the referendum passed," in the words of one anti-tobacco advocate.

Barriers

Several common barriers were identified during the course of our interviews. Many respondents, for instance, indicated that most of the barriers they encountered were political. The chief such barrier appears to be enacting the ordinance in the first place. A number of interviewees held that many of the implementation issues that one might expect to be resolved once the ordinance was passed were actually worked out (or fought out, as the case may be) during the debate over whether the ordinance should be signed into law. In the minds of these interviewees, that process helped create the social norms that are required for the ordinance to be accepted by affected businesspeople and the general populace. In the eyes of many, it is precisely those norms that are responsible for the fact that the ordinances, particularly those related to clean indoor air, are largely self-enforcing.

A second political barrier that was identified during the course of our interviews was that the level of success experienced with one ordinance may dictate whether a city council will attempt to pass a second ordinance. There was a general feeling among some of the interviewees in Flagstaff, for example, that it was unlikely that the city council would attempt to either strengthen an existing ordinance or pass a new one even though their experience with the restaurant ordinance was overwhelmingly positive. As one respondent put it, "In a sense, we are victims of our own success." Apparently, the reasoning goes, once some type of ordinance is passed, council members believe that the problem has more or less been resolved and that it is time to move on to other issues.

In contrast, the rather negative experience with the Tempe vending machine ordinance appeared to increase the likelihood, in the minds of some city council members and other city officials, that a new, and more restrictive, ordinance would be enacted.

A final barrier mentioned on a number of occasions focused on the notion that it was important to spell out the methods by which the ordinance would be enforced. For example, the definitions of restaurants and bars were unclear in the initial Flagstaff ordinance. Similarly, the Tempe vending machine ordinance failed to specify any penalties for noncompliance.

Appendix C

MINNESOTA CASE STUDY

INTRODUCTION

With over 20 years of experience with tobacco control legislation, Minnesota represents a fertile site for study. In a sense, the state provides an opportunity for examining the long-term consequences of an organized tobacco control movement. In short, the state is a "mature market" with respect to tobacco control laws.

In our previous work, we noted that the challenge that confronted the anti-tobacco forces in Minnesota was to keep the smoking issue alive, making it an integral component of both state and local legislators' agendas as well as maintaining the attention of the public at large (Jacobson, Wasserman, and Raube, 1993). To be effective in this regard, anti-tobacco activists faced the task of convincing the state's residents that, despite the passage of the state's Clean Indoor Air Act in 1975 and a spate of local ordinances prohibiting vending machine sales and otherwise limiting teen access to cigarettes, the problems of maintaining smoke-free indoor environments and reducing teen smoking were far from solved.

While the efforts of anti-tobacco activists have met with moderate success in recent years at the state level—including amending the state's Clean Indoor Air Act to contain prohibitions on smoking in schools, day care facilities, and health care facilities and additional restrictions on smoking in restaurants, government-owned buildings, and private work sites—the task of keeping the smoking issue on policymakers' agendas is still at hand.

STATE-LEVEL EFFORTS TO IMPLEMENT AND ENFORCE SMOKING CONTROL LAWS

Synar Amendment

As we found in other states visited during the course of this project, responsibility for coordinating Minnesota's activities related to the Synar Amendment is vested with the agency that is at risk of losing block grant funds. In the case of Minnesota, the responsible agency is the Minnesota Department of Human Services' Chemical Dependency Program Division. Although staff from the division appear to be making a good faith effort to comply with the Synar requirement, they have heretofore had no experience in working with tobacco control issues. As a result, their general strategy has been to contract out to other agencies and organizations that have the relevant expertise.

A central component of the division's strategy has been to introduce legislation that would require local governmental units to enforce the state's statutes prohibiting the sale and distribution of tobacco products to minors. In doing so, local governments would be responsible for licensing tobacco vendors, conducting "sting operations," and reporting the results of these operations to the division. For two years straight, however, the legislation has either failed to pass the legislature or has received the governor's veto.

As a result, the division's Synar-related efforts have been limited to requesting information from cities and counties that have conducted sting operations on the results of those operations, contracting with the University of Minnesota's School of Public Health to conduct a survey of municipalities on their ordinance enforcement activities, and contracting with the Association for Nonsmokers—Minnesota (ANSR) to provide random unannounced compliance checks of vendors in the Twin Cities area. The division has also established ties to the state department of health (McMahon, personal communication).

Division staff argued that their efforts in this regard are limited by federally imposed budget restrictions, which require that states can spend no more than five percent of their block grants on administrative expenses and that any activities undertaken to comply with the Synar requirements must come out of that administrative allocation.

The staff also contend that the rural nature of Minnesota imposes a second constraint, since it is difficult and costly to obtain comprehensive statewide information on programs that local governments have instituted to reduce teen access to cigarettes.

Clean Indoor Air Act

Responsibility for implementing and enforcing the Minnesota Clean Indoor Air Act (MNCIAA) is vested with the Minnesota Department of Health's Division of Environmental Health. Passed in 1975 and amended several times since then, the act either prohibits smoking outright, or restricts it to designated areas, in a broad array of public places. Such places encompass most enclosed, indoor spaces that are frequented by the general public, including private work sites and restaurants.

The department devotes one FTE to coordinating and administering the various provisions of the act. Additionally, it has delegated enforcement responsibility, particularly with respect to restaurants, to over 40 local health agencies. The department enforces the act in all areas where the local health department has not, for one reason or another, decided to participate in the enforcement effort.

By all accounts, the act is largely self-enforcing, and the system remains essentially complaint-driven. According to one staffer, the department receives a total of approximately 100 complaints per year. When a complaint is received, a letter is sent to the business owner outlining the nature of the complaint, describing the requirements of the law, and requesting that the business come into compliance immediately. The department, or the local health agency, then takes no further action unless the individual lodging the initial complaint reports that the violation has not been corrected. If the business fails to comply after the department makes several more overtures, both by mail and, occasionally, by site visit, then an administrative penalty order can be issued. To date, only two such orders have been issued. In one instance, the order succeeded in bringing the offending establishment into compliance and the penalty was forgiven, and the second was under appeal at the time that we conducted our case study.

Interestingly, the comprehensiveness of the state's Clean Indoor Air Act has effectively supplanted the desire of city councils throughout the state to pass ordinances relating to clean indoor air. This effect has chagrined many anti-tobacco activists who believe that while the state law covers a broad range of public places, it is not particularly stringent in the sense that for many public places it simply requires designating particular areas as smoking or nonsmoking. At the same time, it is also interesting to note that while the act has been amended in recent years to include prohibitions on smoking in schools, day care facilities, and health facilities, the tobacco industry has prevented any and all attempts to significantly strengthen major provisions of the act.

ASSIST

Although it is premature to evaluate fully the impact of the ASSIST contract that the state received from the National Cancer Institute on the *outcomes* of tobacco control efforts throughout the state, it is already clear that the contract has influenced the process through which those efforts are carried out. In part, the contract has helped compensate for drastic cuts in the state's tobacco control budget. In fiscal year 1995, ASSIST funds accounted for approximately $1.1 million of the Department of Health's Section on Non-smoking and Health's $1.3 million annual budget. Less than five years earlier, the state devoted $1.6 million to tobacco control activities.

The ASSIST program is in the process of transforming, perhaps radically, the conduct of the state's tobacco control activities. Specifically, the contract has served as a catalyst for shifting the focus of tobacco control proponents from one of public education to policy change. In the words of one of the project's handouts,

> [ASSIST] is a project involving community members and organizations at the local level and the state level to change tobacco policy. . . . The project is focused on tobacco and smoking from an angle that many people are not used to—policy advocacy (Minnesota Department of Health and the American Cancer Society, undated mimeo).

The rationale for this shift, according to the handout, is essentially that while educational services and programs have been valuable in the past, they "tend to be short-lived and only impact a few people at a time." In contrast, policy change "influences larger segments of the population, imparting broad and lasting social change."

The stated goals of the project are as follows: Eliminate environmental tobacco smoke, reduce tobacco advertising and promotion, reduce youth tobacco access and availability, and create economic disincentives to buy or sell tobacco products. The project's basic strategy for achieving these goals involves establishing subcontracts with local coalitions and funding various "special projects." The bulk of the roughly 30 subcontracts that have been made to date have gone to counties, with the remainder going to nonprofit organizations. In some instances, the grants went to preexisting county-based coalitions, while in others new coalitions were formed in response to the availability of grant funds.

The county-based coalitions have typically used the funds as a vehicle for enacting youth access ordinances. According to one interviewee, the coalitions usually conduct comprehensive compliance checks in their respective areas first and then use the results of these checks—which are often less than encouraging—to press for local ordinances that require licensing tobacco vendors, eliminating self-service displays, and so on.

In contrast to other ASSIST states, Minnesota ASSIST has essentially adopted a scatter-shot strategy, which involves making relatively small grants to a large number of coalitions rather than concentrating the grant expenditures on a handful of large-scale projects. In fact, the first round of grants averaged in the neighborhood of $15,000. According to several observers, there is a twofold rationale underlying this strategy. First, in the minds of many anti-tobacco advocates, a small grant is all that is needed to bring a coalition together—to create the "critical mass," as one senior state official put it. According to this model, the coalition will later take on a life of its own, with member organizations making either cash or in-kind contributions to support its activities. Second, a conscious effort is being made in Minnesota to broaden the number of people involved in tobacco control, because previously only a small number of people played any role whatsoever in this area.

Whether the ASSIST strategy selected by Minnesota proves effective remains an open question. Although no formal evaluations of the program have yet been undertaken—in part because the intervention itself runs until 1998—individuals close to the program have reported mixed results. Some such individuals have argued that the program has already had a large impact on city councils throughout the state by getting tobacco control on the agenda, educating local leaders about the hazards associated with environmental tobacco smoke, and creating organizations (i.e., the coalitions) for advancing tobacco control issues. However, a number of individuals hold the view that the ASSIST contracts have thus far produced disappointing results because they have failed to ignite the sense of passion for tobacco control that the contracts' initiators had hoped would materialize.

Prohibition on the Use of Tobacco by Children

According to state law, it is a petty misdemeanor for minors to use, purchase, or attempt to purchase tobacco products. However, this prohibition, which remains controversial, is rarely, if ever, enforced by state or local authorities. Most tobacco control advocates argue that the law is ill-conceived, and that it provides nothing more than a distraction from more serious efforts to limit youth access that attempt to make vendors and the tobacco industry responsible for their actions.

LOCAL EFFORTS TO IMPLEMENT AND ENFORCE SMOKING CONTROL LAWS

After consulting with a number of the state's tobacco control experts, we selected two cities for study: Shoreview and Roseville. Both are Twin Cities suburbs located northwest of St. Paul. In addition, they are both participants in the North Suburban Compliance Project, a group formed by city council members from Roseville, Shoreview, and North St. Paul, as well as the city manager from White Bear Lake and a representative from ANSR. The purpose of this project is to improve compliance with the state law that prohibits the sale of cigarettes to minors.[1] To some extent, the project represents a regional approach to the problem, since all of the participating communities are in the north Ramsey County suburbs. A number of interviewees stressed the importance of adopting a regional approach both out of concern over "border crossing" by teenagers to neighboring communities that do not vigorously enforce the state law and out of equity concerns for merchants.

The project conducts a series of regular compliance checks of all tobacco vendors in the participating communities and reports on the results of the compliance checks to the appropriate city councils. The city councils, in turn, work to develop and refine ordinances that impose sanctions on violators. The ordinances are enforced by local police departments, who also participate in the project.

Relative to results obtained from compliance checks in other communities, both in Minnesota and other states, the project appears to have been quite successful in reducing the number of outlets making illegal sales. According to data provided to the Minnesota Department of Human Services by ANSR, after mounting an educational program for vendors, the baseline rate of illegal purchases in the five original project communities was 25.4 percent. This corresponding figure for the project's second year fell to 19.5 percent (Weigum, 1995). It remains uncertain, however, whether the low illegal sales rates observed in these communities have translated into reductions in teenage smoking rates.

Shoreview

After a false start, the Shoreview City Council enacted a youth access ordinance that, in the minds of many anti-tobacco activists, serves as an excellent model for other communities. The initial ordinance passed by the city council imposed stiff penalties on vendors and required store clerks to be 18 years of age or older to sell cigarettes. In the words of one councilperson, this ordinance "turned out to be a fiasco," because vendors were up in arms and the local police were reluctant to enforce what they considered to be an unreasonable or-

---

[1]Subsequently, a number of other communities have agreed to participate in the project, including Falcon Heights, Maplewood, and New Brighton.

dinance ("the penalty didn't fit the crime," according to one officer). In response, the council amended the ordinance to include a more graduated penalty schedule and to delete the age requirement for clerks. Moreover, the present ordinance contains two penalty schedules: one for vendors who have certified in advance that their employees have undergone a training program that covers the details of the state law and local ordinance and a second, more severe one, for vendors who do not have such training certificates on file.

The ordinance requires that all tobacco vendors be licensed by the city. The license fees, which are $250 per year, are used to conduct merchant education programs and compliance checks. The license may be suspended if the vendor accumulates more than three violations within 24 months. The license fees are intended to make the implementation and enforcement effort associated with the ordinance to be self-supporting. The fees also help ensure that compliance checks are conducted on a regular basis in perpetuity because many observers in the community voiced the opinion that ongoing checks are essential to keep illegal purchases in check.

Several interviewees offered more or less the same set of lessons learned from their experience with the ordinance. First, it is important to get the ordinance right the first time. A number of people felt that they paid a heavy price, in terms of community support, vendor cooperation, and so on, by coming on too strong initially and having to back down. Second, the implementation and enforcement process must be a cooperative one with respect to vendors. City staff took great pains to establish strong lines of communication with the vendors after the initial ordinance was passed, in part to ensure the success of the subsequent one.

Roseville

In several respects, the Roseville ordinance mirrors the Shoreview one. For example, both cities prohibit the sale of cigarettes through vending machines. In addition, the two ordinances both impose penalties on clerks and vendors, and both maintain a penalty schedule that increases gradually with the number of offenses. Perhaps the major distinction between the two ordinances is that Roseville imposes a mandatory two-day license suspension with the second offense within 12 months, a five-day suspension with the third one, and a revocation with the fourth one. The fee charged for a license in Roseville is only a fraction of the Shoreview one, $25 versus $250. Finally, the Roseville ordinance prohibits self-service displays of single packages of cigarettes.

It is interesting to note that the Roseville administrative penalty schedule includes a $50 fine for possession of tobacco products by minors. Yet according to several local government officials, this law is routinely not enforced, largely because the costs of doing so are high. As one interviewee commented, "It is difficult to imagine that one of our local police officers is going to spend an afternoon in the bushes waiting to bust some kids for smoking cigarettes."

Roseville has been reasonably successful in reducing the rate of illegal sales. In less than two years, the fraction of stores caught selling cigarettes to minors dropped from 28 percent to 19 percent. City officials attribute their success to three factors: frequent and comprehensive compliance checks (which have numbered at least two per year since the ordinance was passed); an administrative, as opposed to criminal, enforcement mechanism; and a set of economic consequences that are capable of getting vendors' attention (i.e., license suspensions).

SUMMARY AND CONCLUSIONS

The Roles of Key Stakeholders

Perhaps one of the most interesting aspects of the Minnesota case study is the constantly evolving nature of the roles played by various stakeholders. There are currently several factions that play major roles in the state's tobacco control efforts, including the Smokefree 2000 Coalition, ANSR, and the staff from ASSIST. These factions appear to both compete and cooperate with one another. Additionally, as indicated previously, the influence of the Minnesota Department of Human Services is beginning to be felt in connection with its Synar-related activities. Still, this agency remains very much a secondary player, and one that is viewed by many as having no genuine interest in tobacco control but is simply out to preserve its block grant funds.

The Smokefree 2000 Coalition has mostly concerned itself with issues related to enacting new statewide legislation and preserving the progress that has already been achieved (i.e., fighting the tobacco industry's preemption efforts). Its present focus is on passing a statewide youth access law. Toward that end, however, it has recently devoted itself to supporting local ordinance development, reasoning that such ordinances are a necessary precursor to a statewide bill and that the greater the number of local ordinances, the greater the likelihood that a state bill will be passed that does not contain a preemption provision.

ANSR has played a critical role in both the development of local ordinances and in their implementation and enforcement. Its efforts have received virtually universal positive reviews. A large number of interviewees indicated that ANSR, as opposed to the Smokefree 2000 Coalition, provides the bulk of the leadership on smoking issues and that it has a powerful influence on both state and local officials. Additionally, it has been very active at the local level and has developed a sophisticated ordinance diffusion strategy, which involves everything from selecting target communities that are adjacent to communities that have recently passed ordinances to providing technical assistance to communities and organizing large-scale compliance checks.

For several years now, the department of health has maintained an uneasy relationship with tobacco control advocates throughout the state. While many people give the department credit for obtaining and subsequently administering the ASSIST contract, the department has come under fire for being all but mute on tobacco control issues. In the words of one respondent, "The department has not had a direct voice in tobacco control." As a result, the department has been essentially marginalized by the state's tobacco control community, which instead has looked to the Minnesota Attorney General's Office (which is headed by a Democrat who is often at odds with the state's Republican governor) for leadership.

The tobacco industry maintains a formidable presence in Minnesota, as elsewhere. To a great extent, however, it limits its activities to the state level, where, as noted earlier, it has been successful in turning back major attempts to amend the state's Clean Indoor Air Act as well as blocking efforts to pass a teen access law that does not preempt local ordinances. The strength of the industry's influence at the state level has transformed the strategy adopted by tobacco control proponents into a focus on the local level. As one such individual stated, "Until recently, I felt it would be easy to do things on the state level, but I now believe that you have to do things at the local level because the industry isn't there." That sentiment was echoed by a former city councilman who noted that "the advantage of the local level is that [the tobacco industry] can't get to you because the campaigns don't require large amounts of money."

Barriers

The interviewees identified three major barriers to more effective implementation and enforcement of tobacco control laws. The first was simply that, for reasons that remain largely inexplicable in light of the toll taken by tobacco in terms of morbidity and mortality, the smoking issue lacked the salience that is accorded other issues. As one interviewee bluntly put it, "Smoking is not handguns. As a result, it is often difficult to mobilize people to action." A second respondent indicated that "people don't see tobacco as a threat because they don't see the consequences immediately." And a third said simply that "tobacco control is not a priority for most people."

Related to this is the concern that even anti-tobacco activists in the state appear to focus their attention on enacting new statewide laws and local ordinances rather than on implementation and enforcement issues. One long-time activist in the state lamented that "implementation and enforcement are our weakest points. Nobody is monitoring in a systematic way how the laws we pass are implemented and enforced."

A second barrier revolves around the notion of what many interviewees referred to as "institutionalization," which is essentially the process through which tobacco enforcement becomes part of the general fabric of local law enforcement. There was virtually unanimous agreement on the part of the respondents that regular compliance checks were essential to ensure that vendors refrain from selling cigarettes to minors. At the same time, many individuals expressed concern that such checks would not be carried out in the absence of ongoing financial support. In some instances, such as Shoreview, license fees make the system financially self-sufficient, but even in those instances there is no assurance that the local police department will conduct checks on a regular basis.

Third, while not technically an implementation or enforcement barrier, the fact that the state has been successful in passing a wide-ranging clean indoor air law may have impeded progress in this area at the local level, as communities may believe that clean indoor air ordinances are superfluous in light of the state law. Yet in the minds of many anti-tobacco advocates nothing could be further from the truth because the state law fails to prohibit smoking in a large number of public places and it provides no guarantees to nonsmokers that they will be able to enjoy smoke-free air when frequenting public places.

Relationship Between State and Local Regulation

Minnesota's long history with smoking regulation has generated some important insights into the relationship between state and local tobacco control regulations. One observer of tobacco control regulation in the state has characterized the relationship as a "leapfrog effect," referring to the phenomenon that activity at one level serves as a catalyst for activity at another. For instance, the 1975 passage of the state's Clean Indoor Air Act "built a culture or tone of acceptability" for tobacco control. This, in turn, made it possible for local communities to pass tobacco control ordinances. And now the large number of local ordinances will potentially provide the groundwork for passing a statewide teen access law.

It should also be noted that there appears to be a second dimension to this effect and that is the apparent tendency for local communities to attempt to one-up each other. According to one interviewee, local communities "are willing to go one better than their neighbors and no further." This is perhaps the heart of the diffusion process. That is, it is unrealistic to expect communities to adopt restrictive anti-tobacco laws in a vacuum. Each law must build upon what's been previously accomplished in a given community and in neighboring ones. Clearly, an initial spark is required—in fact, one councilman described his city's ordinance as "spreading like wildfire" once it was passed—but then the process quickly becomes an incremental one in which city council members are almost literally looking over the shoulders of their counterparts in other communities.

Appendix D

CALIFORNIA CASE STUDY

INTRODUCTION

Since the passage of Proposition 99 in 1988—which increased California's cigarette excise tax by 25 cents per pack and used the proceeds to finance tobacco-related education and research programs, media campaigns, and health services—California has been in the forefront of the tobacco control movement. Over the last eight years, a number of significant anti-tobacco laws have been enacted at the state level, which attempt to control teen access to cigarettes and to place restrictions on smoking in public places. In addition, nearly 300 of the state's 468 cities have passed local ordinances to control smoking in public places, including workplaces, and 152 of those cities have passed ordinances that prohibit smoking in all workplaces (Ellis, Hobart, and Reed, 1995).

The results of several opinion polls indicate that tobacco control efforts still enjoy wide public support. For example, 88 percent of the state's residents favor increasing criminal penalties for retailers who sell cigarettes to minors, 86 percent believe that all indoor workplaces should be smoke-free, 85 percent prefer to eat in restaurants that are smoke-free, and 75 percent favor banning cigarette vending machines (California Center for Health Improvement, 1996).

In light of the above, the state presents an interesting opportunity to examine implementation and enforcement issues at both the state and local levels. The plethora of local ordinances complicated our site selection decision somewhat. After talking with a number of long-time tobacco control officials, however, we selected Los Angeles, which had a long tradition of controlling smoking in public places and which passed an ordinance banning smoking in restaurants that preceded AB-13, and Contra Costa County, a Northern California county that illustrates a regional approach toward tobacco control.

STATE-LEVEL EFFORTS TO IMPLEMENT AND ENFORCE SMOKING CONTROL LAWS

Apart from Proposition 99, two significant pieces of tobacco control legislation passed the California State Legislature in recent years. The first is the Stop Tobacco Access to Kids Enforcement Act, which, as the name implies, was enacted in an effort to reduce teenagers' access to cigarettes, and the second is AB-13, which bans smoking in most workplaces.

The California Department of Health Services' Tobacco Control Section serves as the key agency for coordinating the state's tobacco control initiatives. A number of interviewees suggested that the department is focused on what they refer to as the "denormalization" of tobacco use, which essentially involves changing community norms to reflect the notion that tobacco use is socially unacceptable on many different levels, including exposing individuals to environmental tobacco smoke and selling cigarettes and other tobacco products to minors. The denormalization strategy is, in effect, an attempt to marginalize smoking. The concept of denormalization was developed, in part, to contrast sharply with the tobacco industry's notion of "accommodation."

Synar Amendment

The state's primary response to the Synar Amendment was to enact the Stop Tobacco Access to Kids Enforcement Act, or STAKE Act, in 1994, with amendments in 1995. The various provisions of the act prohibit the sale or provision of tobacco products to individuals under 18 years of age, require the department of health services to enforce all laws prohibiting the sale of tobacco to minors, mandate that retailers both check the identification of anyone attempting to purchase tobacco products who appears to be under 18 years of age and to post signs stating that it is illegal to sell tobacco products to minors, and prohibit the sale of tobacco products through vending machines except in businesses that hold liquor licenses. Additionally, the act specifies that the food and drug branch of the department of health services will conduct compliance checks, and that any business owners who are found to be in violation of the law will be subject to civil penalties ranging from $200 to $300 for the first offense to $5,000 to $6,000 for the fifth or subsequent violation within a five-year period (California Department of Health Services, 1995).

Although the food and drug branch is technically responsible for enforcing the STAKE Act and ensuring that the state is in compliance with the Synar Amendment, the Tobacco Control Section of the Department of Health Services plays a strong supporting role by publicizing an 800 number that has been established for the public to report violations, funding approximately 50 merchant educational programs, recruiting youths for compliance checks, and conducting periodic surveys of vendors.

Unfortunately, no data exist on the act's effectiveness, since the regulations implementing the act have only recently been promulgated. However, a 1995 baseline survey of a random sample of 405 cigarette vendors revealed that 37 percent of them were willing to sell cigarettes to teenagers under 18. The results of the survey also indicated that almost half of the gas stations and convenience stores included in the sample were willing to sell cigarettes to underage youths and that self-service arrangements were more likely to be associated with successful purchase attempts in comparison with other arrangements where store clerks distributed the packages (California Department of Health Services, 1995).

Assembly Bill 13 (AB-13)

Enacted in 1994, AB-13 bans smoking in most enclosed workplaces throughout California. Enclosed workplaces are defined broadly to encompass all places of employment, including offices, retail establishments, and restaurants. AB-13, however, exempts small businesses (defined as having five or fewer employees), portions of hotels and motels, large warehouses employing 20 or fewer people, tobacco shops, employee breakrooms designated as smoking areas (provided that they meet certain conditions), and, until January 1997, gaming clubs, bars, and taverns.

AB-13's language regarding preemption is somewhat ambiguous. As a result, tobacco control advocates hold varying opinions on the issue of whether local ordinances can go above and beyond AB-13's provisions and impose more stringent requirements on affected businesses. The consensus appears to be that AB-13 establishes a minimum level of control and that local governments may impose additional restrictions on areas left unregulated by AB-13 (e.g., the workplaces that were exempted under it or areas that are not considered to be "places of employment").

AB-13 requires that the law be enforced at the local level. Specifically, AB-13 mandates that enforcement responsibility be vested with a local law enforcement agency including, but not limited to, local health departments and that the local city council or board of supervisors should determine which agency in a given locale should be charged with this responsibility. According to one observer, the so-called "local lead agencies" selected by cities and counties to enforce the law are for the most part evenly distributed among law enforcement agencies, code enforcement agencies, and city attorneys or city managers.

Under AB-13, a violation is punishable by a fine that may not exceed $100 for the first offense, $200 for the second offense within a one-year period, and $500 for the third and subsequent offenses within a one-year period.

The implementation plan created by the state provides local communities with enormous flexibility in terms of how they elect to implement and enforce the various provisions of AB-13. This general approach has received both praise and criticism from the state's anti-tobacco advocates. On the plus side, a number of interviewees indicated that the approach promotes local control and innovation. However, the approach may create confusion for businesses (particularly small ones) that do business in multiple parts of the state, forcing policy development down to the local level where the required expertise may not reside (e.g., in many instances people who are essentially health educators were asked to deal with code enforcement issues). Also, it may create difficulties for counties to work together, because lessons learned from different implementation strategies may not be transferable across counties.

The counties have experienced varying degrees of difficulty in implementing AB-13. Counties that had not enacted any clean indoor air ordinances or that had enacted weak ones apparently were more apt to have difficulty implementing AB-13 than their counterparts that had some experience with ordinance implementation and enforcement. One observer maintained that the degree of difficulty also varied with community size, arguing that the larger the community, the greater the likelihood that social norms had turned against tobacco.

The level of difficulty associated with implementing AB-13 at the county level was exacerbated by the fact that, in the minds of many interviewees, the California State Department of Health provided very little support. Local tobacco control officials complained that the state provided little or no training to local officials and was late in creating and distributing educational materials. One anti-tobacco advocate argued that the health department's hands were tied by the Republican administration, which tended to placate the tobacco industry, and pointed to one instance where politics prevented the department from putting its name on an educational brochure.

Additionally, many cities are apparently devoting little or no resources to enforcing AB-13, since they view it as yet another unfunded mandate. One Los Angeles–based tobacco control advocate asserted that 25 cities within Los Angeles County alone are intentionally ignoring AB-13. Because the level of enforcement varies across locations, the state still has what one observer referred to as a "patchwork quilt" of protection from secondhand smoke. This matter is complicated by the fact that some anti-tobacco advocates, concerned about efforts made by the tobacco industry to weaken the statewide law, are encouraging local governments to keep existing clean indoor air ordinances on the books rather than revising them to be consistent with the new statewide law (Ellis, Hobart, and Reed, 1995).

LOCAL EFFORTS TO IMPLEMENT AND ENFORCE SMOKING CONTROL LAWS

Los Angeles

Over the course of a 17-year period, the City of Los Angeles passed a series of clean indoor air ordinances prohibiting smoking in a broad range of public places. Taken together, the Los Angeles ordinances closely resembled the provisions contained in AB-13, although the latter has a somewhat stricter set of requirements for workplaces.

The city's restaurant ordinance, which was passed in 1993, prohibits smoking in restaurants, except in bar areas, regardless of where bar areas are positioned within the restaurant. The city attorney's office was responsible for enforcing the entire set of ordinances. Like most communities with similar ordinances, the system was essentially complaint-driven. That is, once a complaint was referred to the city attorney, a letter would be sent to the alleged violator informing him or her that a complaint against them had been received and instructing them about what needed to be done to correct the problem. According to one senior city official, "In virtually every instance the letter was enough to get the problem resolved." In the few instances in which the letter proved to be an insufficient remedy, a hearing was convened between the city and the alleged violator, an exercise that resulted in the resolution of all remaining cases. One of the city's longtime anti-tobacco activists stated that "there was an incredible level of compliance with the ordinance. Nobody had to do anything to enforce it."

After the passage of AB-13, city officials assumed that essentially the identical enforcement mechanism would be used. However, the city attorney's office remarked that they did not have citation authority under California law. Hence, a search was begun for a new enforcement authority. Because the police department was believed to be overloaded with duties that were judged to be more pressing, city officials determined that the fire department was the next logical choice. Since the fire department had recently consolidated some of its inspection function with the Department of Building and Safety, an FTE could be freed up to carry out AB-13–related inspections. Such inspections, however, are only undertaken after a letter has been sent to the alleged violator and a hearing has been held.

Interestingly, several interviewees noted that there was a smooth transition of enforcement responsibility between the city attorney's office and the fire department, and that no tensions arose as a result of the shift.

Contra Costa County

Contra Costa County represents an impressive attempt to develop a regional approach for enacting and implementing clean indoor air ordinances at the local level. As far back as 1984, the voluntary health associations and the County Contra Costa Department of Health founded the Contra Costa County Smoking Education Coalition that, among other activities, developed a model ordinance that was later passed by the county and all of the county's 18 cities. The ordinance prohibited smoking in enclosed public places, a portion of all workplaces, and 40 percent of seating in restaurants that can accommodate 50 or more patrons (Ellis, Hobart, and Reed, 1995). The main advantage of adopting a regional approach is simply that city council members feel "less vulnerable," as one respondent put it, than they would if they independently passed an ordinance. Although the economic arguments against clean indoor air ordinances, especially for restaurants, have not been supported in the literature, they still resonate among some city council members. A regional approach helps blunt the argument by effectively creating a level playing field among neighboring communities.

In the early 1990s, a concerted effort was made to systematically strengthen the ordinances that had been passed in the mid-1980s. With Proposition 99 funding, the county's department of health services started the Tobacco Prevention Project, which provided technical support to cities interested in enacting more stringent ordinances. In 1991, with the help of this project, a group of mayors and county government officials developed a new model ordinance, which was subsequently enacted, in one form or another, and after much resistance generated by the tobacco industry and their front groups, by the county and 16 of the county's 18 cities.

For example, in 1991, Walnut Creek passed an ordinance that prohibited smoking in all restaurants and workplaces and that restricted the placement of vending machines to locations where minors were not allowed. After the ordinance was adopted, the city sent out educational pamphlets to all affected businesses and held informational meetings for restaurant owners. City officials reported that there is a high level of compliance with the ordinance. After more than six years of experience with the ordinance, city officials found that a complaint is received only every few months. On these rare occasions, a letter is sent out by the city attorney's office informing the alleged violator that a complaint was received and instructing them on how to correct the problem. In principle, the police would be sent to cite recalcitrant businesses, but city officials reported that no one has ever been cited under the ordinance.

Several interviewees acknowledged that one of the key factors contributing to the Walnut Creek ordinance's success is that, with respect to restaurants, the enforcement effort is integrated with the health department's biannual inspections. Thus, enforcement is tied into an existing organizational entity.

Another key ingredient for successful implementation and enforcement is educating the public. A number of current and former tobacco control officials in Contra Costa County noted that, as one such individual summed it up, "A huge amount of the enforcement effort is public education, both in terms of the business community and the general public." There is almost universal agreement on the notion that public understanding and acceptance of the ordinance is the critical determinant of its success, and that taking a strong-arm approach—complete with having the local police issue a large number of citations—will prove counterproductive. Toward that end, these officials suggested that brochures on the ordinance be sent out whenever a business license is renewed, that the ordinance contain a provision requiring affected businesses to post signs, and that enforcement authority be vested in a public health, as opposed to a police, agency.

SUMMARY AND CONCLUSIONS

The Roles of Key Stakeholders

In the overwhelming majority of sites visits during the course of this study as well as during the companion one on the political evolution of statewide anti-tobacco laws (see Jacobson, Wasserman, and

Raube, 1993), we commented on the general quiescence of state and local medical societies with respect to tobacco control issues. In California, however, the California Medical Association has been all but vilified by anti-tobacco advocates because of the association's desire to see so-called Proposition 99 funds diverted from tobacco control–related expenditures to pay for medical services to the poor.

As we found elsewhere, the tobacco industry for the most part confined its activities in Contra Costa County to opposing the enactment of the ordinances. Ironically, however, several interviewees suggested that the industry's efforts may have proven counterproductive. As one individual put it, "The tobacco industry provides a target to shoot at. They're the clear villain who has given people a reason to rally." A second observer went even further, stating that "the tobacco industry has had a positive influence [on ordinance development] in some ways."

In addition, there was general agreement among the interviewees that once the local ordinance was passed, and perhaps to a somewhat lesser extent the state-level act, the tobacco industry and other opponents gave up their fight and for the most part did not interfere with implementation and enforcement activities. One observer drew a wartime analogy saying that, "when the war is over, people will say that they'll obey whoever's in charge." He continued, however, to say that "almost always, once the tobacco industry has been defeated, they leave town on that issue, regroup, and come back stronger on the next one."

The state's anti-tobacco coalition was described as "loose" by one member. In general, it comprises representatives from the major voluntary health associations, Americans for Nonsmokers' Rights, and various other organizations, including the California Medical Association, which, as noted previously has recently been at odds with the tobacco control community.[1] From all accounts, the coalition has not played an instrumental role in shaping implementation and

[1]The current state of the coalition appears to be fragile, at best. One observer commented that the issue of how the Proposition 99 funds should be spent "drove a wedge through the coalition." A second offered that the debate over whether the coalition should support AB-13—given the view of some of its members that it was preemptive—created "internecine warfare" within the coalition.

enforcement efforts related both to AB-13 and the STAKE Act, but rather, as we have found elsewhere, has focused its attention on enactment issues.

Barriers

A number of barriers to more effective implementation and enforcement of tobacco control laws were identified by our interviewees. For example, in both Los Angeles and Contra Costa Counties many of the local ordinances failed to specify enforcement mechanisms. As a result, enforcement fell, by default, on the city attorney's office in those communities, which may or may not have viewed tobacco control as a priority issue. A long-time anti-tobacco advocate in the state indicated that it was often the case that after an ordinance was enacted "there was no plan in place for what to do next."

A second barrier noted by a number of individuals concerned the notion that AB-13 has effectively supplanted the desire of local communities to pass ordinances that contain provisions that are more stringent than those found in AB-13 because the city councils believe that the state law has taken care of the problem and/or they are reluctant to go beyond it. One interviewee noted that this phenomenon posed perhaps the greatest potential barrier to providing the state's residents with additional protection from tobacco smoke. He summed up his view by stating that "AB-13 has taken the wind out of people's sails for additional ordinances." This view of the effects of AB-13 is supported by data on the number of local ordinances passed in recent years. In 1993, a total of 68 local tobacco control ordinances relating to both clean indoor air and/or youth access were passed throughout the state; by 1995, the year that AB-13 first took effect, that number dwindled to 12 (Hobart, personal communication).

An official from a statewide health organization indicated that a significant barrier to AB-13's implementation was that the law contains a number of provisions that are vague and difficult to interpret. (This individual cited as an example the way in which the law treats establishments that are composed of both a bar and a restaurant.) According to this observer, the law's ambiguity has caused a number of city attorneys to tell code enforcement officers not to issue citations because, if challenged, they would never hold up in a court of law.

Relationship Between State and Local Regulation

In California, according to one interviewee, the state has essentially followed the lead of local governments with respect to both clean indoor air and teen access. The argument posed by this individual was essentially that if there are enough local ordinances adopted by communities, state policies will be enacted. She added that, "strategically, imposing laws from above is a big mistake." In other words, in California, the large number of local ordinances that were passed by cities and counties throughout the state appears to have created a climate of acceptability for statewide controls. Additionally, the recent defeat of Proposition 188—a tobacco industry–sponsored initiative that would have preempted local ordinances restricting smoking in public places with a weak, statewide law—by California voters indicates that the state's populace supports relatively stringent anti-tobacco measures.

Appendix E

NEW YORK CASE STUDY

BACKGROUND

Summary of Political Evolution

In 1989, New York State enacted one of the nation's strongest statewide clean indoor air acts. The Clean Indoor Air Act (CIAA) was passed after several local jurisdictions had enacted stringent clean indoor air regulations. Subsequently, tobacco control advocates were successful in enacting strong vending machine restrictions in New York City and strong local clean indoor air ordinances in New York City and other downstate localities. In response, the tobacco industry has been lobbying to enact statewide preemption of local ordinances.

Update on Legislative Activity. At the state level, the legislature enacted the Adolescent Tobacco Use Prevention Act (ATUPA) in 1992, with compliance responsibilities shared by the Office of Alcohol and Substance Abuse Services (OASAS) and the New York State Department of Health (NYSDOH). The legislature also enacted the Tobacco-Free Schools legislation in 1994, known colloquially as the Pro Kids Act, which prohibits the sale of single cigarettes ("loosies") and the use of tobacco on school grounds or other youth-related facilities.

At the local level, several stringent CIAA ordinances were enacted in 1994, 1995, and 1996 in New York City, and Nassau, Suffolk, and Westchester Counties. Similar measures are under consideration in

Monroe County (Rochester) and Erie County. In essence, the downstate area is covered by strong local ordinances, while the upstate area is covered only by the state's CIAA.

New York State legislation includes both CIAA provisions and youth access restrictions. Enforcement of both statutes is delegated to local health departments. Under state law, local municipalities can enact and enforce more stringent tobacco control measures, but must coordinate any attempted license removal with the Department of Tax and Finance, which licenses tobacco vendors.

Selection of Local Initiatives. Unlike most other states, New York State offers a wide array of active local enforcement programs. Given resource limitations, we could not select all local municipalities that our respondents suggested that we visit. Based on our conversations with respondents, we selected four local municipalities that represented a range of small, mid-size, and large municipalities that have some geographical distribution. Thus, we visited New York City, Suffolk and Nassau Counties on Long Island, and Chatauqua County in western New York.

Relationship Between State and Local Laws

Unlike preemption states, the relationship between state and local tobacco control laws and agencies in New York State is difficult to characterize. In a sense, they occupy parallel universes with less interaction than we had anticipated. Absent preemption, local municipalities can, and do, enact more stringent tobacco control measures than the state law. And because enforcement is largely delegated to local health departments, the state agencies function more as educational and funding conduits than as close partners in implementing tobacco control laws. The state's tobacco control role is largely educational. Although the Pataki administration appears to be more sympathetic to the tobacco industry's continuing efforts to enact preemption, the tobacco industry has not been able to impose its legislative agenda. Instead, New York retains some of the strongest statewide CIAA and youth access laws in the United States.

In addition, as we describe below, the state's tobacco control regulatory mechanism is highly fragmented, further strengthening any local municipality that wants to undertake aggressive enforcement activities. There appears to be only limited coordination between state and local officials on enforcement activities or strategies. Whatever enforcement occurs is, as we show below, a function of local health department initiatives.

Mirroring the state's bifurcated system, there are both statewide and local anti-tobacco coalitions with different agendas. For the most part, anti-tobacco coalitions have focused their efforts on legislation rather than enforcement.

Several local ordinances are now stronger than the state's CIAA, especially in New York City, Suffolk and Nassau Counties, and Westchester County. The Suffolk and Westchester ordinances were enacted in 1995, suggesting that the experience with the other downstate ordinances was, at a minimum, not a barrier to regional diffusion. One legislator we interviewed argued that

> If the law were a disaster in New York City, then other counties which subsequently enacted ordinances (Nassau and Westchester) would not have followed New York City. Since they went ahead, no-smoking laws can't be too bad.

Nevertheless, between 1989 and 1994, no ordinances were enacted, despite the absence of preemption, and proposed ordinances in Monroe County failed.

IMPLEMENTATION AND ENFORCEMENT IN NEW YORK STATE

State-Level Activity

There are two general themes that characterize the New York State enforcement program. One theme is that enforcement is largely delegated to local health departments.

The second theme is the fragmented nature of implementation responsibilities. No one agency has overall authority or responsibility for tobacco control activities. Even within statutes, enforcement authority is extremely fragmented. For example, OASAS has responsibility for evaluating Synar compliance; the NYSDOH and local health departments have responsibility for ATUPA enforcement, monitoring, and imposing civil fines; while the New York State Department of Tax and Finance has control over licenses. In rural counties not served by a local health department, the district office of NYSDOH enforces CIAA and ATUPA. OASAS also has a separate Synar monitoring function absent enforcement that can be achieved through compliance checks. Though dependent on these other state agencies, OASAS loses federal funds if the state does not comply with Synar. Thus, enforcing ATUPA requires a high degree of cooperation across state agencies.

License removal or suspension can occur only at the state level. If a local health department wants to remove a vendor's tobacco license after repeated violations, it must obtain cooperation from the New York State Department of Tax and Finance.

NYSDOH. There was a trade-off to get the CIAA enacted. At the expense of enforcement, the deal with the legislature was to have local health departments enforce the CIAA. This was subsequently extended to youth access. A major concern expressed by local health departments is that this amounts to an unfunded mandate: "Tell [us] what you want us to stop doing if you want [us] to enforce this." As a result, there is little CIAA enforcement activity—CIAA is self-enforcing and complaint driven, though most places seem to observe the laws.

At best, NYSDOH seems to play a subsidiary role in enforcement activities through the district offices. As noted above, the district offices (DOs) enforce CIAA and ATUPA in rural counties that lack a local health department. For most DOs, enforcement is an afterthought. In fact, the DO does not have independent authority to initiate enforcement but must respond to a complaint.

Two separate local health department respondents characterized the NYSDOH enforcement strategy as "benign neglect." To receive state aid for local public health functions, each county submits a biennial report on its activities, but tobacco control has never been required as part of the general goals before now. For instance, the biannual audit of restaurant inspection programs has not included CIAA inspections. Several respondents argued that the real measure of the state's support will be if the state actually audits for tobacco control efforts and mandates ATUPA compliance measures as part of the local health department's work plan for state aid applications. Tobacco control should be as important to the audit process as the number of hotels and restaurants inspected. Yet these respondents indicated that the state's involvement is better now than it was initially because the state is providing information on ways to conduct a sting and on how to instruct volunteers.

NYSDOH's primary role appears to be as the lead agency for Project ASSIST, a five-year plan to enhance local coalitions. The money originates from the National Cancer Institute and is distributed by the NYSDOH to local coalitions in the form of contracts. All resources are to be allocated to local activities. Starting in 1992, 21 local coalitions have been funded through five-year contracts, with 1995–1996 funding totaling $2 million. Coalitions are required to engage in activities to increase compliance with youth access restrictions, and to advocate for clean indoor air policies. Coalitions are encouraged to supply manpower to local health departments for enforcement efforts.

OASAS. To conduct the requisite ATUPA compliance checks, OASAS has developed a compliance protocol and sampling methodology for a cross-sectional compliance analysis. The goal of Synar is to reduce noncompliance to 20 percent by the year 2000. In each of 25 selected zip code areas, 25 vendors were sampled in July 1996, but OASAS did not collect longitudinal data. Part of the sampling problem is that New York State has very poor information about licensed vendors. Several respondents noted that the New York Department of Tax and Finance's list is outdated and incomplete. OASAS will conduct random compliance checks to develop baseline compliance data. All state agencies receiving the Mental Health Block Grant will participate in the survey.

Responsibility for sales to minors is placed on the vendor; youth possession and use of tobacco products are not penalized. Four strikes at any time and the vendor's license is removed for one year. Three strikes within two years and the license can be removed also for one year. To date, no merchant has had three violations within two years, although several potential violators have been identified in New York City.

ATUPA also restricts the location of vending machines. Respondents noted that the total of vending machines in New York State has declined in the past several years from 12,000 to 6,000.

Local Activity

New York City. The New York City (NYC) Department of Health (DOH) is the primary enforcement agency for all of the laws, but ATUPA enforcement is delegated to the Department of Consumer Affairs (DCA). Stings are conducted by DCA, and ATUPA complaints are referred to DCA. Both DOH and DCA share responsibility for enforcing vending machine restrictions. DOH enforces them during routine restaurant checks and investigates complaints because the NYC vending machine law is more restrictive than the state law. Since there is no ambiguity with vending machines, the law is strictly enforced. All CIAA complaints are sent to the DOH Bureau of Inspections. New York City's youth access law is very similar to ATUPA.

The mayor has supported the ordinance and its enforcement, and even called for a stronger law. Under pressure from restaurateurs, however, the mayor ordered compliance checks to be limited to actual smoking in nonsmoking sections. Thus, DOH is scaling back on procedural violations (signs and ashtrays) by issuing one citation for all procedural violations (thus reducing the overall fine). Yet, there has been no political pressure on DOH from the mayor or the city council to back off from enforcement, although the mayor's support for the law has not necessarily translated into stronger enforcement. In fact, some restaurants, particularly in the outer boroughs, were openly defiant initially. Fines were accepted as a cost of doing business. The mayor then targeted these restaurants with three rounds of nighttime sweeps. About $70,000 in fines were issued from these strikes, now at various stages of the administrative/litigation process.

Based on preliminary data (six months of sweeps through August 1995), nighttime compliance was lower (about 56 percent) than daytime compliance (about 77–80 percent). At this point, DOH is complaint-driven, especially regarding work site compliance. DOH is no longer conducting compliance reviews, save for the restaurant checks that include smoking and vending machine compliance on the inspectors' checklists. According to both industry and city respondents, DOH inspectors support the program.

DCA's primary focus is on stings as the best way to monitor compliance with the youth access law. Usually eight inspectors are assigned to tobacco stings, along with supervisory personnel. Two yearly compliance check rounds are scheduled. About 180 merchants will be targeted in the next round based on previous fines, local busy spots, busy neighborhoods, and word of mouth. It is a convenience sample. DCA has not encountered the same inner city problems as in Illinois (an observation confirmed by other respondents). After coordinating with Heart of Harlem, a community-based anti-tobacco organization, the stings showed an 88 percent compliance rate.

Until recently, statistics on youth access have not been systematically maintained. Four licenses have been removed and available data from October 1995 (including about 20 stores) show a 37 percent compliance rate. Most data are based on stings that focused on signs and loosies. Therefore, early noncompliance rates are higher but are based on process measures. So far, DCA has collected about $100,000 in fines, but respondents do not believe that the program could be self-sustaining on the current $10 city license fee. In April 1996, DCA conducted 196 stings pursuant to the city ordinance. During the stings, 47 percent of vendors illegally sold cigarettes to minors, down from 63 percent in a previous sting. However, 18 vendors violated the ordinance for the third time and face license suspension proceedings.

Suffolk County. Recently, Suffolk County, Long Island, enacted one of the strongest clean indoor air ordinances in the country, with enforcement responsibility delegated to the county health department. The health department is also responsible for the state's CIAA and ATUPA enforcement:

> CIAA is incorporated as part of a broader health department inspection, and most businesses comply with the rules. By not separating tobacco enforcement from other regulatory responsibilities, the county department of health has greater authority to implement and enforce CIAA.

Further, because CIAA is incorporated into their other duties, the county health department has a large pool of inspectors to draw from to enforce CIAA and ATUPA. The county health department estimates devoting two FTEs per year to tobacco enforcement. Perhaps more important, the county health department sees no differences between enforcement and implementation. The county health department is a code enforcing agency that merges education, implementation, and enforcement as one package. For CIAA, the county health department will allow one warning but is less tolerant under ATUPA.

For CIAA, the county health department relies mainly on complaints, except in restaurants, where the health department inspects every facility and mails restaurants the requirements, expectations, and consequences. While complaint trends are stable, fewer complaints are being received about work sites, perhaps because civil norms are "moving in the right direction." The county health department receives many calls asking whether a work site smoking ban is allowable and how to implement one. Nonetheless, one respondent observed that when the department solves one sector, new sectors emerge with lower awareness, and there is no similar smoke-free pattern in restaurants.

To enforce ATUPA, the county health department plans weekly compliance checks randomized by community and by establishment within a community, but this will be difficult to implement. Data on compliance based on stings so far indicate that 55 percent were initially noncompliant, 50 percent were noncompliant during the second round, and 45 percent were noncompliant during the third round. It is, however, a small data set, with a total of 250 checks (80 in each round) out of 2,000 vendors.

> There are short bursts of compliance activity and then regression. The health department needs to conduct random compliance checks 52 weeks per year. Ongoing compliance checks are necessary. It will not be self-enforcing, and there have been no changes in merchants' attitudes.

The evolution of civil norms in CIAA is not apparent in ATUPA. In addition, the respondent said that the county health department had no ability to track smoking prevalence or smoking initiation rates.

Display stands have been a problem for limiting youth access to tobacco. During compliance checks, kids have been able to buy from stores with free-standing displays more readily than from other stores. But the numbers are still too small to draw any conclusions. Anecdotally, having a counter display makes it easier for kids to purchase cigarettes. However, vending machines have not been a problem, mainly because the line-of-sight rules have restricted their presence and use. The strict vending machine law has resulted in fewer cigarette vending machines being used. Gas stations are the single greatest violators. Recent immigrants operate many of them and are "shocked" that you cannot sell cigarettes to minors. Convenience stores and mom-and-pop stores are equivalent violators. Ironically, the best compliance is from tobacco shops because they cannot afford the adverse publicity.

Suffolk County has had greater success in obtaining cooperation from schools than the other local sites we visited. For example, county health department personnel met with school principals at an association meeting and told them that repeat offenders could be referred to the department. Therefore, the department was viewed by the schools as a partner in implementing the law. About 15 kids have been fined modestly ($50) for smoking on school grounds, but only after the fourth or fifth violation and considerable education. Where fines have been instituted, school smoking has declined.

The county health department is developing a pilot program, initiated by the schools as part of the drug-free schools initiative, to identify 70 licensed vendors. They will receive a mailing from the school district reminding them of the law and asking them to "do the right thing." Then, pairs of students (20 volunteers) will visit the merchants and ask them not to sell to kids and will provide signs. Following this outreach and education campaign, all 70 will be stung, though there is no baseline information available for comparison. In the past, six were stung at random, with three sales to minors. The county health department will ask parents and teachers to talk to any remaining violators.

Chatauqua County. Chatauqua County is a small, rural area in western New York. The county department of health enforces both CIAA and ATUPA, allocating 4–5 percent of the environmental health budget to tobacco control. Although the county CIAA predated the state law, they are almost identical. It has been enforced since 1988 but is mostly complaint-based; except for repeat offenders, routine compliance inspections are rare. When the county law was first enacted, the restaurant association feared a loss of business, but it is not complaining now. The county health department receives full support from the commissioner of health, the board of health, and from the inspectors.

According to respondents, community scale is an important factor in how the program is operated. Respondents argued that the county health department is a hands-on operation in a personal, nonadversarial atmosphere, and that the program is successful because the department is able to talk to people. For example, the department talks to every major employer regarding their smoking policy. There is no overt opposition to the program, except on an initiative to eliminate displays, and there is considerable cooperation. In fact, one chain asked for feedback on rewarding clerks (within the store) for not selling to minors. It should be noted, however, that many stores do not even bother to sell cigarettes because of easy access to an Indian reservation near Erie, PA, where cigarettes are exempt from state and federal excise taxes.

Since 1993, the county health department has undertaken ATUPA compliance checks with underage teens and health department investigators. Recruiting has not been a serious problem. The department conducted one warning series, then two sessions in 1994, but not much in 1995. It plans to target about 80–90 stores per year, beginning in 1996. One local legislator is concerned about the erosion of individual rights, but respondents counter that limits on alcohol sales to minors represent a similar erosion and ask why tobacco should be different. Vendors are targeted based on those that have never been checked, have sold to minors in the past, or have received complaints. Fines can range from $100 to $1,000. So far, $500 is the highest fine imposed, but thousands of dollars in fines have been collected.

In conjunction with the local coalition, Chatauqua County has begun a "No Proof/No Puffs" campaign. This is largely an educational effort run by the health department. As in Suffolk County, respondents view enforcement as one part of a broader implementation strategy, even though the law does not include education or implementation: "Vendor education has worked to a degree, but accountability, through enforcement, is required."

Nassau County. Since 1990, Nassau County, Long Island, has had a local clean indoor air ordinance. The county department of health has responsibility for both CIAA and ATUPA compliance, but our interviews suggest that enforcement and implementation are low priorities. One official spends about 5 percent of his time on tobacco control, while another person, hired specifically for tobacco control, was shifted into other duties because of a diminishing workload. Although the number of clean indoor air complaints has been increasing, three years ago the program began doing nothing beyond an initial warning letter to the establishment unless an additional complaint was received. The county health department has not developed any educational materials and has not worked with retail merchants' associations.

There is no active opposition to enforcement. Organized opposition was apparent during public comments on the law, with restaurants being the most vocal. Since then, a respondent has received calls from restaurateurs on how to comply but no calls opposing implementation. Most calls are about workplace and in-office smoking (which is permitted under the ordinance).

In 1995, Nassau County developed a program for youth access compliance. In 1995, 139 stores were targeted, with a 54 percent compliance rate. During 15 tries this year, the compliance rate was 60 percent. The limiting factor in expanding the program is the availability of volunteers. The county health department asked the local coalition for help in recruiting volunteers, without much success. The only ATUPA pressure from the state is to file a report, not to conduct a certain number of stings. Some local police departments are willing to conduct ATUPA stings and willing to issue tickets at the precinct level, but higher officials have objected. Equally important is the lack of personnel to make repeated visits.

STAKEHOLDERS' ROLES IN ENFORCEMENT AND IMPLEMENTATION

Mirroring the fragmented enforcement efforts at the state and local levels, there are two statewide anti-tobacco coalitions and a number of independent local coalitions. They appear to have one thing in common: a focus on legislation and a limited enforcement agenda.

Coalition for a Healthy New York

Anti-tobacco coalitions today represent a much bigger operation than during our previous interviews. In 1989, there was a lobbying coalition with the voluntaries mobilizing local participants. With the beginning of Project ASSIST, the lobbying effort has been more integrated into the activities of the local coalitions. The Coalition for a Healthy New York is a lobbying organization that runs parallel to Project ASSIST (which is run through the New York State Commission for a Healthy New York). According to several respondents, the New York Public Interest Research Group now leads the coalition, in conjunction with the voluntaries, the Parent/Teacher Association, and the League of Women Voters. The New York State Medical Society and the New York State Nurses Association also participate in the coalition. There is considerable overlap between Project ASSIST and the Coalition for a Healthy New York, in part because the local coalitions are interlinked to both the Coalition for a Healthy New York and to Project ASSIST.

The coalition is organized around legislative lobbying, and only sporadically around enforcement. For instance, there is no strategy to generate CIAA complaints. The assumption has been that local Project ASSIST coalitions would be involved in implementation, but the federal government, until recently, restricted their advocacy efforts. As an organizing principle, respondents argued that youth access legislation was unassailable, but the coalition's failure is that it has not yet been successful at organizing to facilitate stings. "Kids' health is still a hot-button issue, but the rise in kids' smoking initiation rates shows the failure of the current enforcement regime."

It is easier for the coalition to focus on legislation where there is a clear victory or defeat. Implementation is much more difficult, and the coalition tends to rely on government. Coalitions are not self-sustaining but need action around a specific problem and a tangible goal to sustain interest, leading one respondent to conclude that "semi-permanent coalitions represent an outdated strategy. Voluntaries, as full-time professionals, must by the watch-dogs involved routinely with local officials."

However, legislation and implementation are intertwined. Several respondents noted that had the coalition recognized the New York

State Department of Tax and Finance's indifference regarding license suspension, it would have pushed for different legislation. In New York, licensure came first, and no thought was given to whether and how licensure would be enforced. The 1992 ATUPA law built upon the existing licensure structure, thinking that the tax and finance department would have an incentive to comply. Unfortunately, there are no complete lists of licensed vendors easily available, resulting in lax enforcement. "Therefore, good enforcement is linked to legislation." All coalition respondents argued that enforcement is more effective and easier to organize at the local level, but according to many respondents, there appears to be less cooperation among the voluntaries than before, except for Long Island.

The New York State (NYS) Commission for a Healthy New York.

The NYS Commission for a Healthy New York, formerly the NYS Commission on Smoking and Health, meets four times per year. At the state level, its activities are political, to influence legislators, the governor, and the commissioner of health. Educational aspects include a Project ASSIST contract overseen by the state health department. A third objective is to establish local coalitions across the state. According to one respondent,

> The most important issue in the world of tobacco is teenage smoking—nothing else is even close. If you stop replacement smoking from teenagers, you stop, or at least limit, the problem. The number of lives saved from youth access restrictions is much greater than through CIAA.

This state commission is interested in enforcement, but it has no money for a scientific study. Project ASSIST funds are not designated for enforcement, and DOH is not prepared to enforce the laws or to spend resources for necessary monitoring. Therefore, there is insufficient information on enforcement.

Local Coalitions

According to our interviews, with the exception of Chatauqua County, the local coalitions in our sample have not been active in enforcement and implementation. As one respondent trenchantly noted, "It is hard to sustain interest in a local coalition after a few meetings or successes. This is an endemic problem with no easy fix." In Nassau County, for instance, the coalition is supportive, but it has deferred to DOH for enforcement and is not involved in generating complaints. When DOH requested help in recruiting ATUPA volunteers, the coalition expressed a willingness to help but provided no actual assistance in producing volunteers. Nor has the coalition pressured DOH to allocate more money to tobacco control enforcement.

In New York City, the Coalition for a Smoke Free City consists of the voluntaries, Smoke-Free Education Services, and the DOH.

> Enforcement is up to the agencies (either state or local). Agencies do not see the coalition as being involved in enforcement. Instead, the coalition is involved in education, such as the Great American Smoke Out and mobilizing public support. [At the local level,] the coalition works as independent entities, with little coalition direction or unified coalition goals. Thus, each member focuses on different issues, with different priorities and goals.

Although in general agreement with this assessment, another coalition participant argued that the coalition was instrumental in focusing on vending machine abuses, leading to greater enforcement and the eventual decline in the number of vendors willing to allow vending machines.

In Chatauqua County, however, the coalition has actively participated in recruiting volunteers for stings, and in educating merchants about cigarette sales to minors. As an external reviewer pointed out, other local coalitions not in our sample also recruit volunteers for stings and provide ETS awareness education.

The Tobacco Industry

By all accounts, the tobacco industry's presence remains primarily at the legislative level, with very little involvement in enforcement and implementation. The exception to this is the tobacco industry's aggressive "We Card" program, aiming to demonstrate the industry's commitment to reducing youth access to cigarettes through vendor participation.

Retail Merchants

In general, retail merchants have not actively opposed implementation and enforcement in New York State. As with the tobacco industry, retail merchants focus on legislative lobbying, especially to obtain preemption. Several officials in local municipalities stated that retail merchants' groups have sent mailings to local merchants asking them to post signs and to become familiar with the laws but are not aware of any training or education conducted by merchants' groups. DCA worked with Philip Morris on a mass mailing to all tobacco vendors. One coalition respondent noted dryly that there is no organized opposition "because the county is too strapped for resources to enforce the laws under any circumstances."

One representative of a local restaurant association argued that the law is complex and selective, allowing restaurants with less than 35 seats to avoid restrictions, along with bar areas. "The law sets up so many different situations, that an imbalance has been created. The law has caused problems because it is selective." His primary argument was to let the market sort it out. As an example of market demand, he cited the "healthy meals" notations on many menus. From this restaurant association's perspective, they are in the hospitality business of accommodating customers. The law puts the association between the smoker and the nonsmoker. "We don't want to be perceived as supporting one group or another. We just want to run our business and take care of customers." Interestingly, he confirmed other respondents' comments that some association members are saying that the law should have eliminated smoking altogether, although he added that members did not report a high demand for nonsmoking seats before the ordinance was enacted.

To the limited extent that respondents noted tobacco industry involvement in enforcement and implementation, the primary opposition strategy appears to be to work through individual restaurateurs and the New York State Restaurant and Tavern Association. The leader of a local restaurant group in New York City holds numerous press conferences and is trying to obtain waivers for 85 restaurants that claim to be losing money because of the ordinance. So far, the group has presented no proof of loss and the Zagat Survey (showing higher restaurant use) refutes this claim.[1] The group has claimed support from two surveys, one from Price-Waterhouse and one from the Cornell Cooperative Survey about restaurant behavior among consumers, but has not released them to the public. Thus, no financial information has been presented with any waiver application.

BARRIERS TO ENFORCEMENT

Our respondents were in general agreement in listing barriers to enforcement shared by clean indoor air and ATUPA. The first barrier is that enforcement is not a high priority with local health departments. School violence, child abuse, and similar issues are more important responsibilities. Local governments are crisis oriented, while smoking is an ongoing problem. The second barrier is resources. Many respondents noted that tobacco control enforcement amounts to an unfunded mandate for local health departments. A third barrier is the lack of coordination between licensure and enforcement. Fourth, the tobacco industry's promotional schemes encourage sales to minors, including displays, slotting fees, ads, and reimbursement for lost sales.[2] Fifth, restaurant owners do not want to enforce the law, nor do waiters because they might lose tips. Sixth, the fine structure in the legislation is a problem. It takes three violations before a license is lost, but with high turnover in ownership (especially at bodegas), this means starting over each time. Also, owners game the system by changing their establishments' names. Seventh, the public is not aware of complaint availability, especially at restaurants, nor is the public aware of the law. Therefore, more public health education is needed.

---

[1]In response to this argument, a local restaurant association representative argued "compared to what?" 1994 had been a "lousy" year for weather, a 21 percent occupancy tax was removed at the end of 1994, and other economic forces suppressed business in 1994. Therefore, the comparison is unfair and not valid because the year would have been a good one no matter what, and we need to await longer-term trends.

[2]Several respondents claimed that cigarette companies routinely reimburse vendors for costs incurred from shoplifting. The reason for reimbursement is to encourage vendors to retain free-standing displays, which are more attractive to teenagers. No respondent produced any clear evidence of this and we were unable to confirm the allegation during our interviews.

ATUPA

Probably the major barrier to ATUPA enforcement in a mid- to large size area is the number of tobacco licensees. In New York City, there are between 15,000 and 17,000 tobacco vendor licensees, making it hard to visit all of them. Also, three "puffs" (violations) are required, which is also hard to do given that store ownership and store names change frequently. In addition, ATUPA needs constant enforcement pressure to be effective. "Merchants benefit too much from cigarette sales to be concerned with local law absent enforcement."

Other barriers include organizing students and protecting their safety, finding kids who are willing to participate ("participants do not think smoking is cool"), getting informed consent, and training them. In some areas, the biggest problem is recruiting kids, but that is not uniform across the sites we visited. The agencies have no qualms about safety, but some parents have worries about safety risks or confrontations with merchants.

CIAA

The fundamental barrier outside of rural areas is the number of venues where smoking may occur. At work sites, smoking is still permitted in private offices, making it difficult for nonsmokers to complain about open doors. Also, workplace and restaurant violations tend to be transient, and thus difficult to enforce. Although the law says that the "customer's demand for a no-smoking section must be met," there is no practical way to operationalize or enforce this absent open flouting of the law by a merchant. More important, there are limited resources, and tobacco control amounts to an unfunded mandate. Nonetheless, respondents argue that while CIAA is self-enforcing, it serves a function as a sentinel—similar to a stop sign at 3:00 a.m.

CONCLUSION

Many respondents in New York State noted changes in the cultural environment since our previous interviews, suggesting that the cultural expectation now is not to smoke. Therefore, several respondents argued that no major enforcement effort is needed for CIAA.

Likewise, a prominent anti-tobacco advocate argued that kids will still have access to cigarettes, just as they have access to alcohol.

> The answer does not lie strictly in enforcement, although vending machines are susceptible to public policy. The future is not through sales enforcement. A two-pronged approach is needed: a pro-health campaign directed to children, and raising the price of cigarettes. Media, public pressure, and price increases are the best strategies.

Appendix F

ILLINOIS CASE STUDY

BACKGROUND

Summary of Political Evolution

In 1989, Illinois enacted a CIAA after a bruising battle that saw the anti-tobacco coalition fracture over whether to accept preemption. Ultimately, a majority of the coalition accepted the compromise, arguing that downstate communities were unlikely to enact tobacco control ordinances in any event.

Update on Legislative Activity. Since passing the CIAA, the major legislative enactment on tobacco control was a 1991 law protecting smokers from discrimination and the 1992 enactment of the Illinois law restricting youth access to tobacco. Like its CIAA counterpart, the law restricting youth access to tobacco was enacted with limited enforcement provisions. Enforcement responsibility was given to the Illinois Liquor Control Commission (ILCC), which already had responsibility for monitoring underage alcohol sales to minors.

Selection of Local Initiatives. Because of the CIAA's provisions preempting stronger local initiatives, our respondents indicated that very few localities had active enforcement programs, limiting the possible local sites. This is especially true for downstate locations. Almost uniformly, respondents suggested Woodridge, a Chicago suburb, and Chicago itself. Although some additional Chicago suburbs were mentioned as possibilities, none had actually conducted a sustained enforcement effort. Thus, we limited our local site visits to Woodridge and Chicago. Woodridge has been studied extensively and has often been cited as a model for local enforcement. Our results are consistent with previous studies.

Neither the CIAA nor the youth access law contains specific enforcement provisions. Chicago has local ordinances on restricting smoking in public places and restricting youth access to tobacco, with enforcement provisions. Woodridge's activities focus on youth access restrictions, using the criminal law and licensure as enforcement tools.

RELATIONSHIP BETWEEN STATE AND LOCAL LAWS

The historical relationship between statewide anti-tobacco legislation and local ordinances can be characterized with relative ease by one word: preemption. Aside from Chicago and its suburbs, there is little local activity. Indeed, state law prohibits local ordinances that are stronger than state law, effectively undermining any sustained local efforts to enact anti-tobacco ordinances. Although local municipalities could expand enforcement activities, it seems clear that preemption undercuts virtually all local tobacco control activity beyond Chicago and its suburbs. For example, ordinances introduced in downstate cities such as Decatur have not been enacted. More important, there is almost no coordination between state and local officials on enforcement activities or strategies. The state's tobacco control role is largely educational.

Our interviews, as detailed below, suggest that the anti-tobacco coalition has focused its efforts on statewide legislation, despite sporadic attempts to enact local ordinances. Our interviews suggest that the tobacco industry and its allies, the retail merchants and restaurateurs, also prefer to fight at the state level. At that level, the tobacco industry is dominant. To be sure, the tobacco industry was unable to stop the Synar legislation (and probably did not want to block it), but it was able to strongly influence which agency would enforce youth access restrictions and how much enforcement authority it would have.

IMPLEMENTATION AND ENFORCEMENT IN ILLINOIS

State-Level Activity

There are two general themes that characterize the Illinois state-level enforcement program. One theme is the absence of statutory enforcement authority. Although the 1989 Illinois CIAA preempts stronger local anti-tobacco initiatives, parallel enforcement authority has not been granted to state agencies. In fact, as noted above, neither the CIAA nor the youth access law provides for state-level enforcement responsibility, essentially delegating enforcement to local agencies. As a result, neither the Illinois Department of Health, with nominal jurisdiction over clean indoor air regulations, nor the Illinois Liquor Control Commission, responsible for youth access compliance, undertakes enforcement activities. As an Illinois Coalition Against Tobacco (ICAT) member observed, "Local health departments are key to enforcement in Illinois. Local health departments in Illinois are autonomous, with loyalty to local politicians."

The second theme is the fragmented nature of implementation responsibilities. No one agency has overall authority or responsibility for tobacco control activities. Under ILCC's five-year youth access plan, for instance, separate departments will be designated as the lead agency for youth access enforcement. The Illinois Department of Public Health (IDPH) will be the lead agency on education, and the Department of Alcohol and Substance Abuse (DASA) will also have limited responsibility for schools. No agency appears to have authority to suspend tobacco licenses.

IDPH. The IDPH's emphasis is on public education, technical assistance, and compliance monitoring rather than enforcement. The education program is designed to "create an environment for public smoke-free expectations." IDPH develops information packets, such as fact sheets, signs, and press releases, that are targeted to specific organizations. Enforcement activity is therefore delegated to local health departments.[1] IDPH is attempting to set program standards for local health departments to include anti-tobacco activity. The current philosophy is for local health departments to conduct needs assessments and use state funds to implement them. However, re-

---

[1]Thus, ICAT works with local officials on enforcement and with the state on education.

spondents at the Chicago Health Department indicated that they have no relations with IDPH on smoking. Respondents added that they "would not know who to call at IDPH." Other local health officials added that

> IDPH will not provide either public or private support if the health department is challenged, and the state provides no funds for enforcement. In short, IDPH is taking a hike at the state level.[2]

IDPH cannot interpret the state's CIAA because it has no rulemaking authority, which is a significant barrier to an active enforcement role. IDPH has not identified any clear-cut compliance areas and looks for other groups, especially ICAT, the statewide anti-tobacco coalition, to take the lead on determining compliance.

Compliance monitoring at IDPH is mostly through phone calls, and mostly done through local health departments. Most complaints have been resolved based on a series of letters, but since IDPH does not maintain statistics about the number of complaints, trend reports are anecdotal. No fines have been issued. As summarized by one IDPH respondent, "CIAA enforcement is dependent on civil norms—it is self-enforcing." Essentially, IDPH relies on voluntary compliance to resolve complaints.

To expand their local enforcement efforts, IDPH is participating in a Centers for Disease Control (CDC)–funded IMPACT program to stress cooperation between health departments and anti-tobacco coalitions. The five-year program was funded in 1994 as a grant to IDPH with ICAT as the advisor. Its primary goal is to implement new policies or strengthen existing tobacco control policies to address the power gap between the people and the tobacco industry. In particular, the goal is to stimulate coalition formation at the local level and thus institutionalize tobacco control activity. IDPH is the program coordinator and will be a resource and training clearinghouse. The training will focus on coalition-building and media advocacy at the local level. The goals are to reduce youth access, improve compliance with the CIAA, restrict tobacco advertising, and develop

---

[2]A subsequent interview suggested that IDPH is now moving to place greater emphasis on tobacco control, including sponsoring conferences and funding one-half FTE for local tobacco control activities. IDPH is also including tobacco in surveys of behavioral risk factors.

local media advocacy with local choice of policy issues. The intent is to provide a community-level (bottom-up) approach to conducting a local needs assessment and using media tools to advance the local tobacco control program.

ILCC. As the agency responsible for youth access enforcement, ILCC is developing a five-year plan[3] that will revolve around offering strategies for local communities to use. ILCC will have no active enforcement role—the agency lacks authority to enforce the anti-tobacco laws. The Illinois youth access legislation called only for a study of tobacco sales to minors, rather than a rigorous enforcement approach.

As part of its implementation strategy, ILCC will be conducting a separate tobacco vendor survey. If tobacco and liquor are sold, vendors will complete a separate tobacco survey. Each vendor with a liquor license is inspected once annually and surveyed at that time. ILCC has no mechanism for identifying vendors that sell tobacco without selling liquor, absence a state licensing requirement. (Liquor licenses are local in Illinois.) Based on preliminary information, 500 municipalities are willing to cooperate in the survey, with 280 willing to conduct stings. In addition to the survey, implementation activities include a video program to teach public officials and county health departments how to conduct inspections with actual purchases. Random, unannounced inspections will be conducted through ILCC using mock purchases. As required by Synar, this will be an evaluative survey to measure if the programs have any effect. Another implementation activity will be vendor education. ILCC will design fact sheets, perhaps using Woodridge as a model. ILCC clearly views education and technical assistance as enforcement techniques and is trying to get the local police to view actual enforcement as "their" issue. But very few local police agencies have conducted formal inspections.

---

[3]According to several respondents, members of the coalition wanted ILCC for youth access enforcement instead of IDPH. In fact, the coalition agreed to leave it with ILCC because not much was likely to be done by either agency. Coalition members also thought that they had a better chance with ILCC because of combining underage alcohol and tobacco sales checks. The tobacco industry did not fight this and now prefers ILCC.

Local Activity

As noted previously, the preemption provision in the state's CIAA limits the incentives for local municipalities to enact separate clean indoor air regulations. Although local municipalities can enforce either the state's CIAA or the state's youth access law, our interviews with knowledgeable respondents indicated that only two local jurisdictions were actively involved in enforcement and implementation activities: Chicago and Woodridge. Most county health departments have not yet included tobacco on the checklist for restaurant inspections.

Chicago. Chicago is a home rule jurisdiction, and its smoking control ordinance was grandfathered in when the statewide CIAA was enacted. The Chicago Department of Health has responsibility for clean indoor air enforcement, while the Chicago Department of Revenue is conducting a demonstration of stings under Synar. The health department has had no communication with the revenue department to coordinate their activities.

The Chicago Department of Health. According to respondents, the current clean indoor air ordinance is somewhat incoherent. For instance, Wrigley Field is nonsmoking out of doors, but the enclosed area is designated for smokers. Another problem with the ordinance is that smokers and nonsmokers have equivalent rights. Thus, restaurants may choose to set aside areas for smokers; otherwise, they should be nonsmoking.

The health department enforces the ordinance on a reactive, case-by-case basis. Most complaints appear to be from nonrestaurant settings, primarily from work sites. The department has conducted no surveys and really has no reliable sense of the number of complaints, although respondents indicated that more complaints have been generated over the past year than before, probably under pressure from ICAT. Most complaints are resolved with some accommodation. However, the department has conducted no trends analyses of smoking complaints. No reports are issued—they simply handle the individual complaint—in part because the smoking complaint system is not automated. To obtain an accurate count, they would need to tally complaints by hand.

The main problem with enforcement is that the ordinance permits designated smoking areas. It is difficult to enforce an ordinance that permits smoking in designated areas because the boundaries and terms are too vague. The ordinance is much easier to enforce if nonsmoking is the norm. The department can revoke a restaurant's license but cannot levy fines for noncompliance. The department's approach is to get proprietors to develop and issue a policy and to enforce it themselves.

The Chicago Department of Revenue. The Chicago Department of Revenue is conducting a pilot study of 120 stores in the city to determine how efficient ticketing merchants is in reducing cigarette sales to minors, and how frequently stings will result in ticketing. The baseline data from previous studies is that 87 percent of underage youths are able to purchase cigarettes without displaying any identification. The study intervention, using actual purchases, consists of ticketing and subsequent education. All inspections occur during regular business hours, though anecdotal evidence suggests that sales to minors are higher in the evenings. Right now, enforcement of laws prohibiting cigarette sales to minors is limited to the pilot (demonstration) program. Cigarettes are part of the regular tax inspection process, but the focus is on cigarette tax stamps and vending machine permits.

The pilot study has produced some interesting preliminary findings. The inspectors find that there is very little communication between merchants regarding enforcement, perhaps because of competitive pressures. Sales rates are similar across demographic regions, but there are indications that merchants are selling cigarettes below the market price to lure customers. In high-crime areas, however, merchants complain that they have other priorities (i.e., survival) than monitoring cigarette sales to minors. In low-crime areas, merchants are more confrontational, complaining that the bureaucrats are interfering by driving business out of the area. One dispiriting result, if true, is that there has been no fluctuation in tax revenue, that is, no aggregate change, despite aggressive enforcement efforts.

For the pilot program, 120 out of approximately 6,000 cigarette vendors in Chicago were inspected. Some stores were inspected every two months, others every four months, others every six months, and there was a control group. Each level (including the control group) received the same educational materials. The sales rates to minors was 25 percent for the two-month group, 40 percent for the four-month group, 60 percent for the six-month group, and 95 percent for the control stores. The initial baseline visit revealed an 80 percent sales rate overall. Out of 270 investigations, 128 vendors sold to minors, and 18 were given no warning. Out of a possible 128 hearings (one for each of the violations), there were only 35 actual hearings. Issues raised by the merchants were entrapment, lack of intent to sell to a minor ("no time to look for customer identification"), and the customer looked older than 21. After a second offense, the merchant's license, either his entire operating license or tobacco license, can be revoked at the department of revenue's discretion.[4]

The pilot program is unlikely to be extended because preliminary results suggest that it is hard to generate sufficient program benefits to justify the enforcement costs. In a city with a high crime rate, it is hard to justify a more expansive cigarette/revenue program.

Woodridge. The Woodridge model of enforcing youth access restrictions to tobacco is perhaps the most studied local municipality in the country. Had there been a suitable alternative, we would not have duplicated these efforts. In general, our results are consistent with those reported elsewhere (see especially, Jason et al., 1996), so our description will be short.

Woodridge determined its own enforcement program on youth access to tobacco independent of Synar or the Illinois CIAA (1989). As a home rule community, it was able to fashion its own approach, at least in youth access matters. The policy adopted by the Village Board is to conduct four inspections per merchant per year. By contrast, Woodridge has no local CIAA ordinance and does not enforce the state law.

Basically, Woodridge has taken a policy position that reducing tobacco use by minors is a priority. People and business generally support the effort. If tobacco use is unchecked at an early age, Woodridge believes that it will lead to long-term substance abuse

---

[4]The fine for a first offense is a 30-day notice to come into compliance. For a second offense, the fine is $200. Hearing results were not available.

problems. As one respondent put it, we "don't want Woodridge to turn into Chicago." Woodridge also takes the position that a license to do business in Woodridge is a privilege, not a right. Merchants must follow the rules, similar to motor vehicle laws. But a constant presence is needed. So far, the program has not been internalized by merchants. The same respondent would expect noncompliance rates to be higher absent enforcement. In fact, he argued that youth access restrictions are not self-enforcing. Instead, noncompliance is treated by some merchants as a minor infraction, "not my problem." Indeed, despite four yearly compliance checks, noncompliance rates varied between 7 and 25 percent in 1994 (which were lower than Woodridge's comparable results for alcohol sales to minors).

So far, no licenses have been revoked, but some have been suspended. Each year, Woodridge issues about 10–15 tickets, with a $25 fine, to children caught smoking. Woodridge does not treat children smoking or attempting to purchase cigarettes as a major offense, in part because kids can quickly dispose of the cigarette. The parental response to the fines has not been negative, and the mayor has received no complaints about this aspect of the program. The basic message to kids is "don't try to buy in Woodridge, go elsewhere."

Despite the national publicity, the Woodridge program has received, it does not appear that the program has diffused much to surrounding communities. At a minimum, there is certainly no coordinated enforcement program across jurisdictions.

STAKEHOLDER ROLES IN ENFORCEMENT AND IMPLEMENTATION

The Illinois Coalition Against Tobacco (ICAT)

The split among the Illinois anti-tobacco coalition members noted in our previous study has not entirely healed. Members continue to cooperate and share a common legislative agenda, but the American Cancer Society is not a formal member of ICAT, which was renamed since our previous study. For purposes of this project, however, our interviews suggest that the split does not at this point affect the coalition's enforcement and implementation strategy. The primary reason for this conclusion is that our interviews consistently revealed that the coalition's primary organizing principle is legislative, with enforcement and implementation as secondary activities.

A typical comment from coalition respondents is

> Up until now, the coalition has not focused on implementation or enforcement. Currently, the coalition remains focused on developing statewide legislation and local ordinances. It is easier for a coalition to rally around legislation than around implementation. Enforcement is a police mentality and could be counterproductive if taken too far.

Another respondent added that "the long-term nature of implementation can be frustrating . . ., advancing only in incremental steps."

More specifically, our interviews indicate that only two individual coalition members are focusing on enforcement at this time. They are currently developing a training manual and workshop for local communities interested in tobacco control enforcement. Implementation is a process of building alliances, but right now, the coalition is more focused on legislation than on building alliances and community support for implementation. The coalition does not have an enforcement strategy, such as generating complaints. According to another ICAT member, "implementation is a second-order concern."

Robert Wood Johnson Foundation (RWJ) Grant

According to several respondents, whatever enforcement and implementation activities the coalition conducts will be conducted through an RWJ Smokeless States grant. The RWJ grant allows the coalition to determine its own priorities among education, prevention, enforcement, media, coalition-building, or policy development (regulatory or enforcement). Each organization can choose a different aspect, such as a grass roots policy. It is a four-year grant to make the community aware that smoking is their issue. One-third of the grant is devoted to enforcement. Another goal is to have the coalition work with state agencies to enforce existing laws. The Illinois Lung Association is interested in the regulatory/enforcement aspects, while the Illinois Heart Association is interested in smoking prevention/cessation. The grant builds the foundation for other activities, such as state legislative action (e.g., trying to raise cigarette taxes). The primary focus is on education and youth access restrictions, with community groups and schools in high-risk areas being the primary targets. The emphasis is in minority communities and on conducting stings. At schools, the grant is focusing on grades three–five through a prevention program.[5] The education program focuses on the criminal outcomes of addiction, pointing out that "this is what the tobacco industry and stores do to our children."

The Tobacco Industry

According to our interviews, the tobacco industry does not play an overt role on enforcement or implementation. Instead, the tobacco industry relies on governmental inertia resulting from the laws' nature as unfunded mandates. There is not much direct tobacco industry opposition to actual enforcement because they can defeat stronger legislation. By limiting the strength of enforcement provisions, the tobacco industry does not need to worry about implementation.

> The skills and money of the tobacco industry are geared up to work the legislative process, but their expertise ends there. Once the issue moves away from legislation and toward professional health care, then supporters of public health enter in, and the tobacco industry is off to the next battle.

Retail Merchants

The Illinois Retail Merchants Association (IRMA) has taken the lead in opposing additional restrictions on youth access, arguing that the legislation is already burdensome to merchants. Their primary argument is that before adding any significant changes in sanctions against sellers, IRMA wants similar sanctions on users—a balance of sanctions against the seller and the buyer. "An underage user should face similar stings, penalties, and public scorn as the retailer if fined or sanctioned." One respondent argued rhetorically, "At what point

---

[5]There is no state law prohibiting smoking in public schools. Several respondents noted that teachers' unions have supported smokers' complaints, arguing that a school must provide a smoking lounge. School districts have not made smoking an issue.

does the responsibility of government and purveyors of legal products stop and the responsibility of parents begin?" IRMA's position is that underage smoking should be treated just the same as underage alcohol consumption.

IRMA also argued that the current fine structure provides sufficient incentives for merchant compliance. What accounts for the high rates of noncompliance, since merchants know the law, are employee turnover and that convenience stores employ teenagers for part-time employment who will not question minors.

Although IRMA opposes local licensing and enforcement, it has cooperated with local officials. IRMA is conducting a limited education program for members that would include window stickers and similar information. The organization is creating a 30-minute video with ILCC and the City of Chicago that will be available to merchants. No merchants' seminars are planned, although IRMA will complete mailings and send informational packets.

BARRIERS TO ENFORCEMENT

With only minor exceptions, barriers to enforcement and implementation detected in our Illinois interviews do not vary between state and local agencies. Thus, except as noted, we will consider them as applicable to both jurisdictions. Not surprisingly, the most consistent barriers mentioned for both CIAA and youth access restrictions are bureaucratic inertia and the lack of resources required to enforce either law. In reality, smoking is a low priority for most agencies.

At the state level, a major barrier is the absence of enforcement provisions in either law. In Chicago, several respondents noted limitations in enforcing both laws in high-crime areas where merchants and restaurateurs fear hostile reactions to tobacco control enforcement.

CIAA

The coalition has been pushing implementation with allies in the Chicago Health Department and IDPH, but both have been confronted with similar arguments—unfunded mandates. The Chicago Health Department is not philosophically opposed to implementation and enforcement, but there are no resources to do so. Outside of Chicago, there is no right to remove a license based on repeated smoking violations. Under any circumstances, the number of work sites and restaurants covered presents an almost insurmountable barrier to rigorous enforcement.

Youth Access Restrictions

Because youth access enforcement in Illinois is at a preliminary stage, our interviews dealt with expected barriers. These include, first, the lack of local police involvement. For the police, this is not a high enough priority. Second, the cost of the program is a potential barrier. A third barrier is the time and resources required to inspect sufficient numbers of vendors. A fourth barrier is that ILCC does not know how to conduct the inspections/stings.

Based on their pilot project experience, respondents in Chicago noted that employee turnover and the low level of employee training were the most important barriers. It may be the law, but the practical side is to look at who is selling the product: minimum-wage, part-time employees who have no stake in avoiding sanctions and who may have an incentive for increasing sales. Respondents added that repeat inspections are the key to obtaining merchant compliance. From the health department's perspective, there is a low return on the inspection investment absent repeat inspections. The health department's statistics indicate that 80 percent of merchants cited for a first offense request a fair hearing, but that there is a much lower hearings request rate following a second infraction. Even so, the health department has concluded that the program has serious financial impediments, and that implementation is not worth the money invested. It requires additional inspection staff, hearings officers and clerks, and the money returned in fines is not all that large. It might require a tax increase to mount the level of effort required. In short, the heavy staff needs make it a hard program to sell.

CONCLUSION

Most respondents in Illinois believe that CIAA is self-enforcing, driven by cultural changes. For youth access, respondents believe that enforcement is necessary and can be effective. In any event, there is little overt enforcement activity, almost none at the state level. Thus, the locus of responsibility for enforcement should be at the local level. To be effective, however, funds would need to be allocated for enforcement. At this point, tobacco control enforcement in Illinois amounts to an unfunded mandate. "Smoking remains a low visibility issue, where state intervention is not taken seriously."

It seems clear, if not unanimous, that the state's enforcement and implementation program is shaped by preemption. For one thing, preemption virtually locks the state into the 1990 law, with little expectation of legislative change at the state level. As a result, there is not much diffusion: "There may be visibility in one area, but there is no place to go." To be sure, preemption does not block local enforcement, but it certainly limits what can be enforced and the sanctions that can be imposed.

Appendix G

FLORIDA CASE STUDY

BACKGROUND

Summary of Political Evolution

With regard to clean indoor air regulations, anti-tobacco advocates have not had an easy time in Florida. In 1985, Florida enacted a weak state law that preempted stronger local initiatives. In subsequent attempts to strengthen the legislation, the tobacco industry was able to attach provisions requiring nondiscrimination against smokers. Recently, however, Florida has joined other states in suing tobacco manufacturers to recover Medicaid costs resulting from smoking. The Florida legislature sustained the governor's veto of legislation designed to end the litigation.

Update on Legislative Activity. The major legislative activities since our previous report have been the state's law in 1992 restricting youth access to tobacco, the Prevention of Access by Children to Tobacco Products Act, and the 1994 Medicaid third-party liability law authorizing litigation to obtain compensation for tobacco-related health care costs. In 1996, the legislature enacted a law prohibiting smoking on, in, or within 1,000 feet of school property.

Florida state legislation includes both CIAA provisions and youth access restrictions. Under both laws, primary enforcement responsibility rests at the state level, although local health departments can enforce the state laws.

Selection of Local Initiatives. Because of the CIAA's provisions preempting stronger local initiatives, our respondents indicated that very few localities had active CIAA enforcement programs, limiting the possible local sites. However, as we discuss below, Florida's youth access enforcement effort is quite active at the state level under Florida's Division of Alcohol, Beverages, and Tobacco (ABT). Our local sites were selected based on youth access activity in three of ABT's field offices after discussions with anti-tobacco coalition members and ABT officials. The local sites selected, Tampa, Miami, and Tallahassee, have active local anti-tobacco coalitions and ABT field offices involved in enforcing youth access restrictions. These local sites are also geographically distributed across Florida, including the state's largest city, Miami, and an area in northern Florida that is largely rural and associated with tobacco growing.

Relationship Between State and Local Laws

As in Illinois, the historical relationship between statewide anti-tobacco legislation and local ordinances can be characterized with relative ease by one word: preemption. There is little local activity, and our interviews revealed virtually no attempts to enact local ordinances, except in West Palm Beach. Indeed, state law prohibits local ordinances that are stronger than state law, effectively undermining any sustained local efforts to enact anti-tobacco ordinances. Although local municipalities could expand enforcement activities based on state law, it seems clear that preemption undercuts virtually all local tobacco control activity. Thus, there is almost no coordination between state and local officials on enforcement activities or strategies.

IMPLEMENTATION AND ENFORCEMENT IN FLORIDA

State-Level Activity

The absence of any local enforcement activity places the burden of enforcement on the responsible state agencies. With regard to youth access restrictions, there is a sustained enforcement effort. For the CIAA, the state largely relies on voluntary compliance. As in most states in our sample, enforcement responsibility is fragmented across various agencies, with little communication or coordination regarding strategies, goals, or methods.

HRS. The Department of Health and Rehabilitation Services (HRS), the state agency responsible for enforcing the state's CIAA, relies exclusively on public complaints to enforce the act.[1] Until recently, HRS had only one position for the entire state to enforce the act, but now a second position has been added. The enforcement program is funded by the health care block grant, not out of HRS funds. The agency has done nothing with local governments and has no formal working relations with the Florida Department of Education on shared materials.

The system is entirely complaint-driven—there is no compliance review follow-up. All HRS respondents noted a trend toward voluntary compliance but provided no support for this statement. The agency can order and achieve compliance, but the real question for HRS is the cost of enforcement. While HRS can request the environmental unit of a county's HRS to investigate a complaint, enforcing the sanitation code is the state HRS's primary responsibility.

Most complaints occur at work sites, but there are no clear complaint trends. The Division of Business and Professional Relations regulates CIAA compliance at work sites, not the department of health. Complaint levels and targets show considerable fluctuation, but the respondents were not willing to share much data. In fact, no trend analyses have been conducted. Most cases are resolved after the first warning letter following a complaint. The agency's policy is that fines will be negligible, to be used as a means of last resort.

The agency's implementation strategy has not changed much over time. HRS focuses on broad implementation rather than rigorous enforcement. HRS complies with the legislative authority and nothing else. For instance, the agency only provides education in helping vendors to understand what the law requires. "Nothing beyond that is within the agency's purview." Agency representatives will attend

[1]Since our interviews, the legislature has created a separate department of health. While we do not know how this change will affect the anti-smoking enforcement effort, one respondent indicated that the Health Promotion Office is now part of the Communications Office, suggesting greater attention to tobacco control activities.

meetings but will only speak about the law and what the compliance requirements are. For example, the agency works closely with the Tri-Agency Coalition (see below), but there is no official interaction "because the agency runs on specific authority, but the coalition has diverse agendas."

Although the state's CIAA enforcement mechanism appears to rely almost entirely on voluntary compliance, it is important to point out that coalition respondents believe that HRS has been responsive within the limits of their resources. Thus, many respondents believe that the law has had some impact despite low enforcement levels. Initially, some entities went beyond the law, including some airports and the Chancellor of the University of Florida. At airports, there has been some retrenchment from earlier compliance levels, and when administrators refuse to comply (such as in the Orlando Airport), one person at the state level cannot ensure compliance.

ABT. By all accounts, ABT, the designated enforcement agency for youth access restrictions, has aggressively moved to reduce cigarette sales to minors. Indeed, tobacco enforcement is a priority for ABT, being one of its strategic goals. "ABT has invested considerable manpower, money, and time in the program." As a regional director noted, "A committed agency is a necessary condition for enforcement."

While there is no set number of inspectors for each district, ABT maintains that each district has adequate manpower to enforce the law. Within overall command policy, the district offices have considerable operational flexibility. As a buy-in, strategic plans are developed by field managers, and ABT uses an incentive system in performance reviews for inspectors to earn points for tobacco enforcement. Points can be earned for recruiting kids or for making sting attempts/arrests/administrative cases. One respondent admitted that this is controversial among agents.

The ABT's strategic plan calls for each of the district offices to sting 80 percent of tobacco vendors. Tobacco vendors are selected based on previous information (i.e., complaints). Under recent policy guidance, random stings using underage operatives are also allowed. ABT's policy is that if a vendor sells to a minor during a random test, the vendor will first be issued a strong warning. The vendor receives a notice of a violation for the second offense. For the third offense, charges are filed against the license or permit. No vendor has gotten to that point yet, but some have two offenses already. When a violation is found, ABT's policy is to go back within two weeks to see if the violation continues, by checking different shifts. The case is closed if the repeat visit finds no problem, but if a subsequent complaint is filed, the vendor will be treated as a repeat offender.

At three recent strikes, ABT recorded a 20 percent noncompliance rate, when it expected 60 percent noncompliance. (In fact, one of the regional offices we visited showed a 65 percent compliance rate, with considerable fluctuation. For instance, on some days, seven out of nine vendors are out of compliance.)

Before an administrative action for sales to minors will be initiated, a vendor must have three strikes. For vending machine violations, only one strike is needed to proceed to an administrative hearing. So far, no licenses have been revoked. In a 1994 ABT survey, 1 percent of retail vendors were checked, with 540 violations, 10 administrative cases, and a 19 percent noncompliance rate. At three recent stings, ABT recorded a 20 percent noncompliance rate, but other offices showed a 35 percent noncompliance rate.

Under the Vendor Responsibility Act, a vendor can mitigate a violation if certain programmatic elements are in place, such as employee training or meetings with employees. The vendor needs to document these elements. To assist vendors, ABT engages in an education program where inspectors provide signs, knowledge of the law, and methods to ask for identification. ABT will also participate in training employees. Nevertheless, licensure is an important component of the enforcement program. Vendors respond to business costs, not to criminal enforcement.

In general, large chains have better compliance rates than small merchants (and there is some indication of partnerships forming between chains and ABT). Large chains have better training programs, but even there, one of six attempted buys by a teenager may result in a sale. Chains have a computer program at the point of sale reminding clerks to ask for identification—it operates as a red flag. However, there is a manual override, with clerks often replying "I don't know why," when asked why they sold to minors without checking identification. The computer program may work over time, but results are mixed, given high employee turnover.

Local police agencies can also enforce over-the-counter tobacco sales to minors, although few have done so outside of joint demonstrations with ABT. Respondents indicated that local officials look to the state for tobacco enforcement, especially since only the state can bring an administrative action for license removal.

Although not unanimous, our respondents noted that the field directors have received positive feedback from field officers. One reason for the positive response may be ABT's appeal to law enforcement officers that tobacco control is a law enforcement issue consistent with ABT's overall mission. However, one respondent pointedly observed that not all agents view tobacco use by minors as a problem justifying ABT's time and attention.

ABT expects all vendors to comply, including inner-city merchants—there are no exceptions. ABT does not intentionally avoid any vendor, although it is harder to recruit volunteers in the inner city.

Vending Machines. Florida law now requires that tobacco vending machines be within the proprietor's line of sight, that is, the responsible employee's sight, or removed altogether. A citation is issued for a first offense, a $500 fine. ABT field offices have disseminated information to vendors about the line of sight requirement. The industry has responded by pressuring merchants not to remove the machines, but to put them within the vendor's line of sight. Unlike New York, where there appears to be a decline in the number of vending machines, ABT respondents reported no fewer vending machines in this area than before Synar. "Cigarette vendors are helping to make sure that vending machines are within the clerk's line of sight."

STAKEHOLDER ROLES IN ENFORCEMENT AND IMPLEMENTATION

The Tobacco-Free Florida Coalition

As in Illinois, the statewide anti-tobacco coalition has been renamed but has not entirely healed from the searing dispute over preemption and nondiscrimination provisions in the 1990 CIAA. As one close observer noted, "There is still lots of competition between the voluntaries, although there is no open split." In fact, the American Cancer Society is not a formal member of the new coalition, Tobacco-Free Florida (TFF), although their goals remain congruent and they cooperate at the legislative level. For purposes of this project, however, our interviews suggest that the split does not at this point affect the coalition's enforcement and implementation strategy. The primary reason for this conclusion is that our interviews consistently revealed that the coalition's primary organizing principle is legislative, with enforcement and implementation as secondary activities.

Our interviews suggest that TFF is likely to focus on implementation activities, such as education, while deferring to public agencies to enforce the laws. In short, TFF has no strategies for enforcement, such as local surveys of restaurants or pressure on local businesses. Several respondents argued that "implementation is not part of the coalition's agenda." Education followed by information is the coalition's primary agenda after legislative advocacy. A major activity is to organize local coalitions to contact local legislators.

To date, the local coalitions we visited seem to be focused on media strategies. For example, the Tampa-based coalition has a grant from RWJ to conduct a media campaign in Pinellas and Pasco Counties. The campaign focuses on community education regarding youth access to tobacco, raising questions such as what are the laws and how should the public be educated. According to respondents, people are not aware what the laws are, thus the need to emphasize community education. The coalition views education as a much less intrusive way of dealing with the problem. So far, the local coalition has not expended much effort on implementation or enforcement.

As an organizing strategy, the coalition is emphasizing youth access restrictions. TFF hopes to empower youth to take on the tobacco industry. An additional plan is to increase teacher awareness of tobacco control issues through teacher training on tobacco. In Dade County, however, the coalition has received little cooperation from schools.

> Schools do not place a high priority on restricting smoking. In particular, SCAT [Student Coalitions Against Tobacco] has not been

> embraced by the schools. Especially in inner city areas, schools are overwhelmed by curriculum demands.

The coalition structure in Florida is somewhat complex. The Tri-Agency Coalition (composed of the three voluntary associations) still operates with TFF at the state level. But Tri-Agency sets the legislative agenda, which is then adopted by TFF. Under TFF, there are six local advocacy coordinators that are tantamount to separate local coalitions. This is a new program started in 1994 with RWJ funds. Each coordinator needs to build and educate coalition members. Even at this level, the priority is to explain the legislative agenda to new members, even though the legislative agenda is set by TFF. Except for legislation, each local coalition has complete autonomy to set its own agenda, based on guidelines supplied by the TFF coordinator.

However, the advocacy coordinators have had trouble focusing their efforts so far. Thus, the local coalitions have not yet focused on a few select initiatives to be pursued, such as cooperating with ABT on youth access enforcement and on encouraging the establishment of smoke-free restaurants. At this point, the local coalitions have not played an active role in enforcement or implementation, although one local group in Pensacola worked with ABT to obtain youth volunteers for enforcement stings. In addition, local coalitions need to establish their own priorities and raise money to implement them. Our interviews suggest that local coalitions will have a difficult time achieving either of these objectives. In particular, as one respondent stated, "unless some foundations contribute, it is hard to see how most of the local coalitions as structured will be able to raise money."

Although several respondents were critical of TFF, it is important to remember that the reconstituted coalition had been in existence for less than two years when these interviews were conducted. Nevertheless, some of the problems noted by respondents pertain to structure rather than execution of a strategy. For example, one typical observer noted that the coalition

> is too large in structure and activities, with six working groups at the state level: schools, communities, health care, work sites, media, and policy. But it has not been easy to operationalize the working groups, as they are hard to galvanize and coordinate at the state

level. It is easier to organize around a locally identified target than at the state level.

The Tobacco Industry

The tobacco industry's primary strategy appears to be to hang onto preemption. There is no indication that the industry is active at the local level or is attempting to undermine enforcement or implementation efforts. In schools, the industry is promoting "We Don't Want Kids to Smoke," that smoking is an adult habit or choice. Other than organized opposition to the state's litigation against tobacco companies to recover Medicaid costs, there has been no organized tobacco industry response to implementation.

Retail Merchants

For the most part, retail merchants do not appear to be involved in enforcement and implementation activities. TFF and the local coalitions report little communication with retail merchants' associations, and the associations do not appear to provide educational materials on tobacco control for their members.

Initially, ABT received complaints from retail merchants that the stings amounted to entrapment but now reports receiving cooperation from merchants on over-the-counter sales. As one ABT field officer noted, "No one wants to be on record as OK to sell to minors, so there's a limit on industry pressure." Opposition to vending machine restrictions remains an issue. Some retailers, however, have removed their vending machines instead of a fine, but no numbers were available.

Our interviews with retail merchants associations indicate that members are not complaining about enforcement and are voluntarily complying with the clean indoor air laws. The general trend in retail is toward no smoking, but the issues are more difficult and controversial in restaurants. One association representative expressed the organization's philosophy as follows: "If nonsmokers do not articulate their opposition, then tough—the audience is never wrong. It is not incumbent on the owner to read the customer." Depending on the attendant enforcement responsibilities on businesses, his organization might not oppose a formal ban; members want the issue decided one way or the other.

BARRIERS TO ENFORCEMENT

Most respondents noted that the major barriers to enforcing tobacco control laws are the lack of resources, preemption, and the lack of public awareness and education. Aside from the educational barrier, which coalitions can address, no one indicated that the other barriers would change any time soon.

Youth Access Restrictions

According to one observer,

> No matter how hard the investigation, kids will continue to buy cigarettes and alcohol—kids will obtain them. Because there are no statutory provisions against possession, there is no way to get to the juvenile. We can make all the sales arrests and it won't affect sales to minors. Absent sanctions for possession, there are no sanctions to stop the behavior [similar, he argued, to car theft, juvenile delinquency, and alcohol consumption].

In justifying other enforcement priorities, one regional ABT field officer noted that cigarettes cause harm to individuals while alcohol may kill (through drunk driving).

Just as important, one regional ABT director commented that there needs to be a sanction against vendors and merchants for the program to work. The criminal court's approach is "light," relying on plea bargains. Thus, the judicial system is a barrier to enforcement. Several actual buys are required to show a pattern before the merchant will be sanctioned. Obtaining the necessary three strikes is a laborious process. If the merchant is adequately training staff about tobacco sales restrictions, courts will rule that there are mitigating circumstances and will not impose a fine. In alcohol enforcement, it is a violation to solicit sales to minors, but there is no analogue in tobacco sales. In short, the department is willing to enforce the law, but the courts do not take it seriously, limiting legislatively imposed sanctions.

It is also hard to recruit kids for stings. Stings are labor intensive, and ABT has no money to pay volunteers. Parents do not want kids to be involved (presumably for safety concerns). One field office has only had one referral from the coalition. There have been some complaints, but there is a lack of public knowledge about the tobacco laws, and public apathy. Thus, ABT must rely on random inspections.

CIAA

The major barrier noted by respondents is preemption. As in Illinois, preemption limits local agency willingness to enforce the law, deferring to the state. At the local level, "there is a feeling of hopelessness because they cannot do anything." Preemption thus undermines the ability to organize around a local ordinance—"it gives away the house and stifles local initiative." "Tobacco control advocates need to reframe the issue to one of local control."

Several respondents indicated that an important CIAA barrier is that people are not aware of the law, of the right to file a complaint, or of the HRS 800 phone number. If so, these facts would tend to justify the coalition's focus on media and educational strategies. One state official was even skeptical that levels of enforcement would make a difference, maintaining that

> stronger penalties and a larger enforcement staff would not have made a difference, and there is no evidence that they are necessary. CIAA is either self-executing or it will not work, which is similar to other public health efforts. Generally, the population is ahead of the bureaucrats.

CONCLUSION

One of the coalition's most experienced lobbyists argued that the most effective use of the coalition's time and resources would be to seek stronger legislation rather than implementation and enforcement. For example, clerks, individuals, and restaurants do not want to enforce smoking restrictions and anger customers. A store will thus ignore a CIAA violation. This reluctance to enforce CIAA restrictions can be overcome with fines so that the store has more to lose than the customer.

Most respondents agree that the CIAA will be self-executing through community values. "People will basically follow CIAA, and it is hard to determine what the state would do beyond what it is already doing." For example, it is hard to issue a ticket or citation for smoking—local law enforcement agencies could write citations but are unlikely to do so. This also raises the (unwelcome) specter of the smoking police. In short, neither the state nor the local coalition is engaged in formal activity to enforce CIAA.

CIAA is therefore self-executing (or is not executed at all). The absence of a local enforcement entity certainly appears to discourage the coalition from monitoring compliance. But this seeming reliance on government acts to the detriment of organizing a vital coalition response around implementation and enforcement.

More than in any other state in our sample, the issue of penalizing youths for possessing cigarettes is a major topic of discussion in Florida. Most respondents favoring this position wanted a small fine or community service requirement rather than a criminal statute. Each of the ABT respondents mentioned the advisability, from an enforcement perspective, of penalizing both a merchant and the minor for illegal cigarette purchases. So far, the coalition has steadfastly opposed this approach, although some coalition members expressed general agreement with it.

Appendix H

INTERVIEW GUIDE FOR ASSESSING THE IMPLEMENTATION OF TOBACCO CONTROL LAWS

I. BACKGROUND

A. History of Site's Tobacco Control Initiatives

1. Restrictions on minors' access (e.g., prohibiting sale/distribution, vending machines)
2. Restrictions on smoking in public places
3. Other tobacco control laws
4. Distinguishing features of site that may limit or enhance generalizability

B. Current/Most Recent Initiatives

1. Perceptions of factors that motivated most recent initiative
2. Goals of legislation/ordinance
3. Components of laws (i.e., coverage provision, nature of restrictions, etc.)
4. Plans to meet requirements of Synar Amendment
   - (a) Responsible agency
   - (b) Unannounced inspections conducted
   - (c) Report to the Secretary of Health and Human Services
   - (d) Activities carried out

(e) Extent of success in reducing availability of cigarettes to minors

(1) measures used to determine success

(2) data collected or analyzed

(f) Enforcement strategies for coming year

II. IMPLEMENTATION, ENFORCEMENT, AND DIFFUSION PROCESS—TEEN ACCESS AND REGULATIONS RESTRICTING SMOKING IN PUBLIC PLACES

A. Legislative Implementation, Enforcement, Diffusion Provisions

1. Where is authority for carrying out each of these provisions vested?

2. Budget for carrying out required activities

3. Evaluation requirements

4. Implementation goals and process

B. Implementation, Enforcement, and Diffusion Strategies

1. Role stakeholder plays/has played

(a) Historical role in developing, implementing, and enforcing anti-tobacco laws

(b) Current and future role

(c) Stakeholders' perceptions of roles of other key participants in the development/implementation/enforcement process (including legislators, health agencies, police, school officials, tobacco industry lobbyists, coalitions, media, medical society, and voluntary health associations)

(d) Do people implementing the ordinance/legislation redefine its objectives?

2. Dissemination methods

(a) Process of disseminating laws/ordinances to the public

(1) Media campaigns

    (2) Materials distributed
    (3) Diffusion across municipalities
  (b) Resources allocated to education, dissemination of state laws or local ordinances
    (1) Materials distributed
    (2) Special materials for schools
    (3) Special materials for vendors to minors
  (c) Media activity to publicize restrictions

3. Enforcement methods
  (a) Responsibility for enforcement
  (b) Reliance on self-enforcement and "civility norms"
  (c) Do municipalities/states with more stringent ordinances/laws enforce them to a greater extent than areas with less stringent ordinances/laws?
  (d) Is there a sentinel effect of enacting law/ordinance, regardless of enforcement effort?
  (e) Do states target activities to communities with no local ordinances?
  (f) Complaints received, warnings and citations issued, reports of violations, distribution of offenses, recidivism rates
  (g) Sanctions imposed
  (h) Sting operations
  (i) Removal of vendor licenses (probably a state function)
  (j) Fines (to minors or vendors)
4. Changes in implementation strategies over time
5. Analysis of strategies
  (a) Evidence of noncompliance (i.e., media reports of "fights" over smoking)

(b) Evidence of voluntary restrictions (e.g., workplace restrictions) in absence of or stricter than law/ordinances require

(c) Surveys on public attitudes toward law/ordinances

(d) Studies showing costs and benefits of anti-tobacco laws or enforcement activity (state and local levels)

(e) Other activity to reduce availability of cigarettes to minors

C. Barriers to Effective Implementation, Enforcement, and Diffusion

1. Political
2. Economic
3. Social/cultural

III. RELATIONSHIP BETWEEN STATEWIDE ANTI-TOBACCO LEGISLATION AND LOCAL ORDINANCES

A. Historical Development of Relationship

1. Salience of teenage smoking at state versus local levels
2. Preemption attempts

B. Strategies of Coalitions and Other Anti-Tobacco Advocates—Past, Present, and Future

1. Actual or predicted tobacco industry response

C. Locus of Enforcement Resources

D. Evidence on the Relative Effectiveness of the Two Approaches

E. Spillover Effects at Local Level

IV. ROLES OF ANTI-TOBACCO COALITIONS AFTER ENACTMENT OF LAWS

A. Role and Mission of Coalition with Respect to Implementation and Enforcement

1. How do coalitions organize to implement and/or enforce laws (overall and for teenagers)?
2. Changes in coalition role following enactment
    - (a) Ability to raise money
    - (b) Ability to sustain membership
    - (c) Specify actions taken or planned to pressure businesses or authorities to enforce laws (i.e., monitoring activity)
    - (d) Measures of success/effectiveness
    - (e) Activities in schools
3. Explore relationships between state and local coalition activity
4. Activity across municipalities
5. Effects of preemption on local activity
6. Effects of strong statewide legislation on local activity
7. Data collected/studies undertaken
8. Explore diffusion issue
9. Do coalitions attempt to cooperate with affected business interests once laws are enacted (adversarial relation during legislative process and cooperative during implementation)?

B. Resources Devoted to Implementation and Enforcement

1. Grants, assistance from national organizations, etc.

C. Nature of Relationship Between Coalitions and Affected Businesses

D. Methods for Improving Implementation and Enforcement Process

V. STRATEGIES OF OPPONENTS TO BLOCK OR UNDERMINE IMPLEMENTATION AND ENFORCEMENT EFFORTS

A. General Strategy of Various Opponents (e.g., Tobacco Industry, Vendors, Restaurateurs) Regarding Implementation/Enforcement

B. Contributions of Opponents to State/Local Organizations, Sponsoring State/Local Sporting Events

C. Materials on Selling to Minors Distributed to Association Members

D. Tobacco Industry Activity (Advertising, Materials Distributed) to Discourage Sales to Minors

E. Lobbying Regarding Laws/Ordinances Restricting Sales to Minors (e.g., Vending Machine Restrictions)

F. Formal Challenges to Restrictions

G. Studies Conducted

H. Response to ETS Findings

I. Level of Cooperation Among Groups Opposed to Legislation/Ordinance

J. Establishment of Local "Smokers' Rights" Groups

VI. MISCELLANEOUS ISSUES

A. Comments on Selection of Local Sites

B. Other Potential Interviewees

C. Sources of Documentary Evidence

BIBLIOGRAPHY

Altman, L.K., "The Evidence Mounts on Passive Smoking," *The New York Times*, May 29, 1990.

Americans for Nonsmokers Rights, *Counts of Local Smoking Control Ordinances*, data provided to this project, Americans for Nonsmokers Rights, Berkeley, Calif., May 1996.

Arizona Department of Health Services, *A Report on Youth Access to Tobacco: Results of the ADHS Tobacco Pilot Programs*, Arizona Department of Health Services, Phoenix, Ariz., 1995.

Bierig, Jack R., Susan A. Weber, and T. Robert Scarborough, " Legal Analysis of Approaches to State and Local Regulation of Tobacco Advertising and Sales in the US," prepared by Sidley and Austin, Chicago, Ill., at the request of the American Medical Association, 1994.

Brownson, Ross C., James R. Davis, Jeanette Jackson-Thompson, Joan C. Wilkerson, "Environmental Tobacco Smoke Awareness and Exposure: Impact of a Statewide Clean Indoor Air Law and the Report of the US Environmental Protection Agency," *Tobacco Control 1995*, Vol. 4, 1995, pp. 132–144.

Buchholz, Patricia, "Legal Aspects of the Control of Tobacco," *Legal Medical Quarterly*, Vol. 4, Spring 1980, pp. 14–30.

Burns, D.M., et al., "Report of the Tobacco Research Study Group on Smoke-Free Indoor Air Policies," *Tobacco Control*, Vol. 1 (Suppl.), 1992, pp. S14–S18.

California Center for Health Improvement, *California's Anti-Tobacco Strategy,* California Center for Health Improvement, Sacramento, Calif., 1996.

California Department of Health Services, "Summary of Tobacco Laws Controlling Tobacco Sales and Distribution to Minors," mimeo, California Department of Health Services, Tobacco Control Section, Sacramento, Calif., 1995.

Centers for Disease Control (CDC), "The Surgeon General's 1989 Report on Reducing the Health Consequences of Smoking: 25 Years of Progress (Executive Summary)," *CDC* 38 (Suppl. No. 2), 1989.

Centers for Disease Control (CDC), "Minors' Access to Tobacco—Missouri, 1992, and Texas, 1993," *Morbidity and Mortality Weekly Report (MMWR),* Vol. 42, 1993a, pp. 125–128.

Centers for Disease Control (CDC), "Mortality Trends for Selected Smoking-Related Cancers and Breast Cancer—United States," *MMWR,* Vol. 42, 1993b, pp. 857–861.

Centers for Disease Control (CDC), "Cigarette Smoking Among Adults—United States, 1992, and Changes in the Definition of Current Cigarette Smoking," *MMWR,* Vol. 43, 1994, pp. 342–346.

Centers for Disease Control (CDC), "State Laws on Tobacco Control—United States, 1995," *MMWR,* Vol. 44 (Suppl. No. SS-6), November 3, 1995a.

Centers for Disease Control (CDC), "Minors' Access to Smokeless Tobacco—Florida, 1994," *MMWR,* Vol. 44, November 20, 1995b.

Centers for Disease Control (CDC), "Tobacco Use and Usual Source of Cigarettes Among High School Students—United States, 1995," *MMWR,* Vol. 45, 1996, pp. 413–418.

Chaloupka, F.E., *An Economic Analysis of Addictive Behavior: The Case of Cigarette Smoking,* doctoral dissertation, City University of New York, N.Y., 1988.

Christoffel, T., and S. Stein, "Using the Law to Protect Health: The Frustrating Case of Smoking," *Medicolegal News,* Vol. 7, No. 4, 1979.

Coalition on Smoking OR Health (CSOH), *State Legislated Actions on Tobacco Issues,* Washington, D.C., 1993.

Coalition on Smoking OR Health (CSOH), *State Legislated Actions on Tobacco Issues,* Jessica Bartelt, ed., 1995.

Coconino County Department of Public Health, *Flagstaff Tobacco Use Prevention Program Summary Report,* Flagstaff, Ariz., 1995.

DiFranza, J.R., and L.J. Brown, "The Tobacco Institute's 'It's the Law' Campaign: Has it Halted Illegal Sales of Tobacco to Children?" *American Journal of Public Health,* Vol. 82, No. 9, 1992, pp. 1271–1273.

DiFranza, J.R., J.A. Savageau, and B.F. Aisquith, "Youth Access to Tobacco: The Effects of Age, Gender, Vending Machine Locks, and 'It's the Law' Programs," *American Journal of Public Health,* Vol. 86, 1996, pp. 221–224.

Doegey, J., and D. Barber, *Local Regulation of Smoking and Vending of Tobacco Products—Tobacco Politics Reaches Arlington, Texas,* paper presented at the NIMLO annual conference, Arlington, Tex., 1994.

Elders, J.M., C.L. Perry, M.P. Eriksen, and G.A. Giovino, "The Report of the Surgeon General: Preventing Tobacco Use Among Young People," *American Journal of Public Health,* Vol. 84, No. 4, 1994, pp. 543–547.

Ellis, G.A., R.L. Hobart, and D.F. Reed, "Overcoming a Powerful Tobacco Lobby in Enacting Local Smoking Ordinances: The Contra Costa County Experience," unpublished manuscript, 1995.

Emont, Seth L., Won S. Choi, Thomas E. Novotny, and Gary A. Giovino, "Clean Indoor Air Legislation, Taxation, and Smoking Behavior in the United States: An Ecological Analysis," *Tobacco Control,* Vol. 2, 1993, pp. 13–17.

Feighery, E., D.G. Altman, and G. Shaffer, " The Effects of Combining Education and Enforcements to Reduce Tobacco Sales to Minors," *Journal of the American Medical Association (JAMA),* Vol. 266, No. 22, 1991, pp. 3168–3171.

Garner, D.W., "Banning Tobacco Billboards: The Case for Municipal Action," *JAMA,* Vol. 275, 1996, pp. 1263–1269.

Glantz, S.A., "Editorial: Preventing Tobacco Use—the Youth Access Trap," *American Journal of Public Health,* Vol. 86, 1996, pp. 156–157.

Goggin, M.L., *Policy Design and the Politics of Implementation: The Case of Child Health Care in the American States,* University of Tennessee Press, Knoxville, Tenn., 1987.

Hobart, R., *Americans for Nonsmokers' Rights,* memorandum with attachments to Jeffrey Wasserman, March 12, 1996.

Institute of Medicine (IOM), *Growing Up Tobacco Free,* National Academy Press, Washington, D.C., 1994.

Jacobson, P.D., J. Wasserman, and K. Raube, "The Politics of Anti-Smoking Legislation: Lessons from Six States," *The Journal of Health Politics, Policy, and Law,* Vol. 18, 1993, pp. 787–819.

Janerich, D.T., and D.W. Thompson, "Lung Cancer and Exposure to Tobacco Smoke in the Household," *New England Journal of Medicine,* Vol. 323, No. 10, 1990.

Jason, L.A., W.D. Billows, D.L. Schnopp-Wyatt, and K. King, "Long-Term Findings from Woodridge in Reducing Illegal Cigarette Sales to Older Minors, *Evaluation and the Health Professions,* Vol. 19, 1996, pp. 3–13.

Jason, L.A., P.Y. Yi, M.D. Anes, and S.H. Birkhead, "Active Enforcement of Cigarette Control Laws in the Prevention of Cigarette Sales to Minors," *JAMA,* Vol. 266, No. 22, 1991, pp. 3159–3161.

Kagan, R.A., and J.H. Skolnick, "Banning Smoking: Compliance Without Enforcement," in *Smoking Policy: Law, Politics, and*

Culture, Robert L. Rabin and Stephen D. Sugarman, eds., Oxford University Press, New York, N.Y., 1993, pp. 69–94.

Kagan, R.A., and D. Vogel, "The Politics of Smoking Regulation: Canada, France, the United States," in *Smoking Policy: Law, Politics, and Culture,* Robert L. Rabin and Stephen D. Sugarman, eds., Oxford University Press, New York, N.Y., 1993, pp. 22–48.

Keeler, T.E., et al., *Taxation, Regulation, and Addiction,* Working Paper No. 91-173, Department of Economics, University of California, Berkeley, Calif., 1991.

Kingdon, J.W., *Agendas, Alternatives, and Public Policies,* Little Brown and Co., Boston, Mass., 1984.

Kluger, R., *Ashes to Ashes: America's Hundred-Year Cigarette War, the Public Health, and the Unabashed Triumph of Philip Morris,* Alfred A. Knopf, New York, N.Y., 1996.

Lewit, E.M., M. Botsko, and S. Shapiro, "Workplace Smoking Policies in New Jersey Businesses," *American Journal of Public Health,* Vol. 83, 1993, pp. 254–256.

Lewit, E.M., D. Coate, and M. Grossman, "The Effects of Government Regulation on Teenage Smoking," *Journal of Law and Economics,* Vol. 24, 1981, pp. 545–570.

Marcu, Stephen E., Seth L. Emont, Ruth D. Corcoran, Gary A. Giovino, John P. Pierce, Michael N. Waller, and Ronald M. Davis, "Public Attitudes About Cigarette Smoking: Results from the 1990 Smoking Activity Volunteer Executed Survey," *Public Health Reports,* Vol. 109, No. 1, January–February 1994, pp. 125–134.

Mazmanian, D.A., and P.A. Sabatier, *Implementation and Public Policy,* Scott Foresman and Company, Glenview, Ill., 1983.

McDonnell, L., and R.F. Elmore, *Alternative Policy Instruments,* JNE-03, RAND, Santa Monica, Calif., 1987.

McGinnis, J.M., and W.H. Foege, "Actual Causes of Death in the United States," *JAMA,* Vol. 270, 1993, pp. 2207–2212.

McLaughlin, M. "Learning from Experience: Lessons from Policy Implementation," *Educational Evaluation and Policy Analysis,* Vol. 9, 1987, pp. 171–178.

McMahon, M.J., Minnesota Department of Human Services, memorandum with attachments to Jeffrey Wasserman, June 9, 1995.

Minnesota Department of Health and American Cancer Society, background information on Minnesota ASSIST, undated mimeo, Minneapolis, Minn.

Natale, T., "Cigarette-Machine Measure Fizzles," *Arizona Tribune,* December 29, 1994.

National Cancer Institute (NCI), *The Impact of Cigarette Excise Taxes on Smoking Among Children and Adults,* August 1993.

Nordstrom, D.L., and F. DeStefano, "Evaluation of Wisconsin Legislation on Smoking in Restaurants," *Tobacco Control,* Vol. 4, 1995, pp. 125–128.

Palumbo, D., and D. Calista, "Opening Up the Black Box: Implementation and the Policy Process," *Implementation and the Policy Process,* D. Palumbo and D. Calista, eds., Greenwood Press, New York, N.Y., 1990.

Patten, Christi A., John P. Pierce, Shirley W. Cavin, Charles C. Berry, and Robert M. Kaplan, "Progress in Protecting Non-Smokers from Environmental Tobacco Smoke in California Workplaces," *Tobacco Control 1995,* Vol. 4, 1995, pp. 139–144.

Pressman, J.L., and A. Wildavsky, *Implementation,* University of California Press, Berkeley, Calif., 1976.

Rabin, Robert L., "Some Thoughts on Smoking Regulation," *Stanford Law Review,* Vol. 43, January 1991, pp. 475–496.

Radecki, T.E., and C.D. Zdunich, "Tobacco Sales to Minors in 97 U.S. and Canadian Communities, *Tobacco Control,* Vol. 2, 1993, pp. 300–305.

Rigotti, Nancy A., David Bourne, Amy Rosen, John A. Locke, and Thomas Schelling, "Workplace Compliance with a No Smoking

Law: A Randomized Community Intervention Trial," *American Journal of Public Health,* Vol. 82, No. 2, February 1992, pp. 229–235.

Rigotti, N.A., and C.L. Pashos, "No Smoking Laws in the United States: An Analysis of State and City Actions to Limit Smoking in Public Places and Work Places," *JAMA,* Vol. 266, 1991, pp. 3162–3167.

Rigotti, Nancy A., Michael A. Stoto, Michael F. Brier, Amy Rosen, and Thomas Schelling, "Retail Stores Compliance with a City No-Smoking Law," *American Journal of Public Health,* Vol. 83, No. 2, February 1993, pp. 227–256.

Rigotti, Nancy A., Michael A. Stoto, Mark Kleiman, and Thomas Schelling, "Implementation and Impact of a City's Regulation of Smoking in Public Places and the Workplace: The Experience of Cambridge, Massachusetts," Institute for the Study of Smoking Behavior and Policy, JFK School of Government, Harvard University, Publication No. S-88-17, January 1988.

Rigotti, Nancy A., Michael A. Stoto, and Thomas Schelling, "Do Businesses Comply with a No-Smoking Law? Assessing the Self-Enforcement Approach," *Preventative Medicine,* Vol. 23, 1994, pp. 223–229.

Samuels, B.E., M.E. Begay, A. Hazan, and S.A. Glantz, "Phillip Morris's Failed Experiment in Pittsburgh," *Journal of Health Politics, Policy, and Law,* Vol. 17, No. 2, 1992.

Samuels, B.E., and S.A. Glantz, "The Politics of Local Tobacco Control," *JAMA,* Vol. 266, 1991, pp. 2110–2117.

Schwartz, G.T., "Tobacco Liability in the Courts," in *Smoking Policy: Law, Politics, and Culture,"* Robert L. Rabin and Stephen D. Sugarman, eds., Oxford University Press, New York, N.Y., 1993, pp. 131–160.

Sciacca, J., "A Mandatory Smoking Ban in Restaurants: Concerns vs. Experience," *Journal of Community Health,* Vol. 21, No. 2, 1996.

Sciacca, J., M. Ratliff, and P. Pappas, "Prohibiting Smoking in Restaurants: Effects on Restaurant Sales," unpublished manuscript, Flagstaff, Ariz., May 1996.

Slattery, M.L., L.M. Robison, T.K. French, T.M. Abbott, J.C. Overall, Jr., and J.W. Gardner, "Cigarette Smoking and Exposure to Passive Smoking Are Risk Factors for Cervical Cancer," *JAMA*, 1989, Vol. 261, p. 1593.

Sylvester, K., "The Tobacco Industry Will Walk a Mile to Stop an Anti-Smoking Law," *Governing*, May 1989, pp. 34–40.

Texas Department of Health, Office of Smoking and Health, *City Nonsmoking Ordinance Survey*, Texas Department of Health, Austin, Tex., 1991.

Tollison, R.D., and R.E. Wagner, "Self-Interest, Public Interest, and Public Health," *Public Choice*, Vol. 69, 1991, pp. 323–343.

U.S. Department of Health and Human Services (USDHHS), *The Health Consequences of Smoking, Cancer: A Report of the Surgeon General*, USDHHS, Atlanta, Ga., 1982.

U.S. Department of Health and Human Services (USDHHS), *The Health Consequences of Involuntary Smoking: A Report of the Surgeon General*, USDHHS, Rockville, Md., No. 87-8309, 1986.

U.S. Department of Health and Human Services (USDHHS), *Preventing Tobacco Use Among Young People: A Report of the Surgeon General*, USDHHS, Atlanta, Ga., 1994.

Wagner, S., *Cigarette Country: Tobacco in American History and Politics*, Praeger, New York, N.Y., 1971.

Warner, K.E., "State Legislation on Smoking and Health: A Comparison of Two Policies," *Policy Sciences*, Vol. 13, 1981.

Wasserman, J., W.G. Manning, J.P. Newhouse, and J.D. Winkler, "The Effects of Excise Taxes and Regulations on Cigarette Smoking," *Journal of Health Economics*, Vol. 10, 1991.

Weigum, J., *Association for Nonsmokers—Minnesota*, memorandum with attachments to Phil Brekken, May 10, 1995.

Winter, S. "Integrating Implementation Research," in *Implementation and the Policy Process,* D. Palumbo and D. Calista, eds., Greenwood Press, New York, N.Y., 1990.

Zellman, G.L., A.S. Johansen, and J. Van Winkle, *Examining the Effects of Accreditation on Military Child Development Center Operations and Outcomes,* MR-524-OSD, RAND, Santa Monica, Calif., 1994.

Zycher, B., *Insurance Markets, Smoking, and the Coase Theorem,* paper presented at Annual Meeting of The Western Economic Association International, San Diego, Calif., June 30–July 3, 1990.